RUBBING SHOULDERS

RUBBING SHOULDERS

The Story of a Rugby Prop

Phil Blakeway
with Chris Ducker

Stanley Paul
London Melbourne Sydney Auckland Johannesburg

Stanley Paul & Co. Ltd

An imprint of Century Hutchinson Ltd

17–21 Conway Street, London W1P 6JD

Hutchinson Publishing Group (Australia) Pty Ltd
PO Box 496, Hawthorn, Melbourne, Victoria 3122

Hutchinson Group (NZ) Ltd
PO Box 40–086, Glenfield 10, Auckland

Hutchinson Group (SA) Pty Ltd
PO Box 337, Bergvlei, 2012 South Africa

First published 1985

Phototypeset in 11/12pt Linotron Baskerville
by Input Typesetting Ltd, London

Printed and bound in Great Britain by Anchor Brendon Ltd,
Tiptree, Essex

British Library Cataloguing in Publication Data

Blakeway, Phil
    Rubbing shoulders: the story of a rugby prop.
    1. Rugby football—England
    I. Title
    796.33'3'0924   GV945.9.G7

ISBN 0 09 162860 1

Contents

To Ros, Laura and James

Acknowledgements

For permission to reproduce copyright photographs the author and publishers would like to thank Colorsport, Associated Sports Photography, Mike Brett, Bob Thomas Sports Photography, *Daily Express*, Gloucestershire Newspapers and Sporting Pictures (UK) Ltd.

I should like to thank Chris Ducker of the *Bristol Evening Post* for all his assistance in putting together my story. With our mutual interest in west country rugby, we had a good starting point, and it proved most enjoyable working together.

Foreword

If it had been my good fortune to play every match with a prop forward of Phil Blakeway's quality, I would not now be the possessor of such splendid cauliflower ears!

Phil is often described as the cornerstone of England's Grand Slam side in 1980. And that's exactly what he was. Indeed, I would describe him as possibly the best tight head I had the pleasure of pushing behind during my entire career.

Our first meeting was on the somewhat ill-fated England tour of Australia in 1975. We were both raw recruits to international rugby – as it probably showed on the field – and neither of us set the world on fire.

I was lucky enough to win my first cap on that trip and then become a regular member of the England team. But Phil had to wait another five years to gain recognition, everyone quite wrongly assuming that a promising career had come to an end when his neck was broken during a Gloucester club game in 1977.

By 1980, Phil was back, the selectors very shrewdly picking him for the Rest XV in an England trial. Although Phil scrummaged very well on that day, it was still a surprise when he was chosen for a debut against Ireland.

I well remember the reservations expressed at our first practice session together when the newcomer was lifted by the opposition front row. Phil turned to me apologetically and said he wasn't used to second rows shoving so hard! He promised it would not happen again – and it didn't.

Phil was really the crucial last piece in the jigsaw as far as the formation of the Grand Slam side was concerned. With his great friend and mentor Fran Cotton moving to the loose head, he filled the one glaring weakness at tight-head prop.

Quite apart from his mighty efforts up front, Phil did me a considerable favour that season against France at Parc des Princes. A French forward took a dislike to me and there's no doubt I was in imminent danger of taking some severe punishment as I lay trapped on the ground. Phil stepped in to protect me and was kicked so hard that he suffered a broken rib.

It's a measure of the man that, despite this injury, he played in the next two internationals, staying on for the sake of the team against Scotland after receiving another blow on the same spot. This was a truly heroic performance.

Without doubt, Phil Blakeway was one of the most loyal and respected of players in the Grand Slam side. He also gave great service to England in the years which followed. May I wish Phil and his family every success in the future.

Bill Beaumont

1

Bump and Grind

The pre-match luncheon before England faced Wales at Cardiff in April 1985 was a wonderfully nostalgic affair. It had been organized by my old Gloucester front row comrade-in-arms Mickey Burton – rugby's Mr Fix It – and many of the great players I battled with and against over the years were there.

I should have been winning my twentieth England cap that afternoon. But in order to play against Scotland and Ireland during March, I had needed to pump myself full of drugs to ease constant back and neck pain.

After returning home from Dublin, a visit to Gloucester Royal Hospital (over the years, I've acquired a season ticket for their X-ray department!) confirmed the worst. While once before I had survived a broken neck in a Gloucester club game and made a successful comeback, two vertebrae were seriously damaged this time. Even consultant orthopaedic surgeon and ex-Commonwealth Games athlete Ray Davies – so reassuring on previous occasions – felt it would be sensible to call it a day.

Suddenly, therefore, my career was over. Quitting wasn't perhaps the disaster it might have been – because it was the fourth time that I had announced my retirement.

The first, not surprisingly, was after the broken neck in 1977. In 1981, I called it a day because of a back problem and the fact that I no longer had the will to cope with what I called the 'bump and grind' of rugby. Retirement number three came the following year after a row with a Gloucester official who felt – totally without justification – that I wasn't putting enough commitment and dedication into my club rugby.

In 1985, however, there was no going back. Burton's Cardiff shindig was for former internationals . . . and the convivial company soon made it remarkably easy for me to accept my new status.

Burton himself had loomed large in my life since the day some fifteen years before when I propped against him for my first club Cheltenham, in one of the annual scraps against Gloucester, which I subsequently joined in 1971.

Appropriately, the luncheon guests included Bill Beaumont who cajoled and inspired the England team of 1980 to a glorious Grand Slam. I have no hesitation in stating that my international career was built, quite literally, on the shoulders of the skipper. Propping in front of Bill was like sitting in an armchair – you took up position and waited for the supercharged Sherman tank in the second row to do the rest.

The lads in the Grand Slam side jokingly described me as the 'Little West Country swede basher' – mainly because most of them were from the North and Midlands.

The Cardiff gathering included the hooker from that team, Peter Wheeler. Also there was Welshman Derek Quinnell, captain on the day in East London, South Africa, when I made my one and only appearance for the British Lions. Present, too, were three of the most respected Welsh front-row forwards of all time – Charlie Faulkner, Bobby Windsor and Graham Price.

'Put that lot together and you would have a pack good enough to win this afternoon,' suggested one Welshman wryly.

The day would have been perfect had England ended their long-standing Cardiff jinx and slammed the Welsh. Home supporters didn't rate their team good enough to lace the boots of a few Welsh sides of recent years. Unfortunately, someone forgot to remind the optimistic English that Wales always tripled their efforts against the red rose. We lost 24–15.

I felt sad for the boys and particularly for the chairman of selectors, Derek Morgan, so desperate for a win before taking the side out to New Zealand. The dentist from Newbridge had been responsible for resurrecting my international career against Rumania during the previous January, remembering that, despite being known primarily as a tight-head prop, I could still do a reasonable job on the loose head as well.

On his advice, England took the enormous gamble of picking me on the strength of just one senior game for Gloucester in the first half of the season (and that as a tight head). Derek was prepared to rely on what he had seen five years earlier, when Gloucester recalled me after injury to play loose head at Pontypool – and we won.

If I have any lasting regret, it is that a broken rib deprived me of any hope of representing the Lions in a Test in 1980.

On the other hand, I enjoyed so much success – a John Player Cup win, County Championship final glory with Gloucestershire, the Triple Crown and Grand Slam with England, plus Barbarians' selection. And I did at least qualify as a Lion. I think it's right to say that no other English player can claim such a record.

In my early days I was one of rugby's bad boys – I don't mind admitting it. I was sent off playing for both Cheltenham and Gloucester and in 1975 a Rugby Union president told me I was such a disgrace to the game that I would never wear an England shirt again. Over the years, however, you mellow and learn to appreciate the exhilaration of the sport when it is played hard and fair.

But rugby is a physical game and there are always occasions when you have to stand up and be counted. I have known many big, very fit men who, when the knuckle started, were found wanting. Sometimes, you must get involved and, as the great Fran Cotton used to say, 'Meet the challenge.'

Fran, as this book explains, had a very considerable influence on my career. What a player he was! His father had been a Rugby League hooker for twenty years – one of the grafters of the northern game – and could never understand why his son should have preferred Rugby Union.

But Fran obviously inherited the grit and dedication of a professional and is as straight as they come. He was a fitness fanatic and sound technician and would never dream of taking a short cut in training. 'If the buggers cheat now, they'll do it in the match,' he insisted. 'When the coach says run round the corner, it means run round the corner.'

Obviously, there are formidable pressures on and off the field for any international rugby player. But my philosophy has always been, 'If you don't like it, get out of the firing line.'

Watching England at Cardiff, I could only admire the stoicism of twenty-year-old Rob Andrew, who could well be an outstanding international player for years to come. In his debut against Rumania, the fly-half had been barracked by the Twickenham crowd while he kicked at goal. Against France he was subjected to some very rough handling and, after a second and third late tackle, I thought he was certain to go off. But the lad stuck it out. Clearly, he will cope with the pressures.

Why then, I wondered, would someone like Eddie Butler, captain of Wales on numerous occasions, decide to jack it in because, as he explained, people were getting at him too much? If I had worried about what was said to me, I would have finished long ago. His departure from the scene merely meant that someone else would come along and win a Welsh cap – and revel in it. So who is the loser? Eddie Butler. Perhaps he is more sensitive than me. On the other hand, how can you be sensitive and play for Pontypool?

I think to stay at the top you need the sort of ruthless, rather selfish streak that has driven me on at various critical periods of my career. Sometimes, perhaps, I've taken it too far – but my wife Ros has patiently and resolutely stood by me throughout.

We were married at Down Hatherley, Twigworth, near Gloucester, in May 1973 and have two children – Laura, born in 1977, and James, two years later.

The time just before Laura's birth will never be forgotten because Ros was eight months' pregnant when

I broke my neck playing against South Wales Police in a Wednesday evening game at Kingsholm.

The extent of the damage was not discovered until the following weekend *after* I had completed a County Championship match for Gloucestershire against Cornwall at Camborne. Eventually Ros – not exactly feeling 100 per cent fit herself – drove me to Gloucester Royal Hospital and I wince now when I think how every cat's eye in the road felt like a mountain.

Once there, we were greeted by a doctor who had been on duty for forty-eight hours virtually without sleep. How grateful I am that he still had the patience to look with such scrupulous care at the X-rays and conclude that there was enough evidence to treat my case as a broken neck. It seems astonishing to me that a man who had endured such long hours at work could be asked to make decisions which, in some instances, might mean life or death. That, quite literally, was how serious my case could have been.

I was in a big neck brace when the time came for Laura's birth and the hospital staff seemed more concerned about the possibility of the new father fainting, falling from the stool and finishing himself off. When Laura finally popped into the world, she was passed over to me but, because of the position of my head, I couldn't look down and see the babe in my arms. They had to sit me in a lower chair so that I could cuddle her properly for the first time.

It was a very sobering moment. Here were Ros and I experiencing the greatest event of our lives and yet I could, at the very least, have been paralysed and helpless.

The weeks which followed were enough to test the strength of any marriage. I was not a great deal of use around the house and so Ros had to cope with my needs and those of a tiny infant. It was a long time before life returned to anything resembling normal routine.

Only the down-to-earth players of Gloucester Rugby Club could have taken my subsequent return to the game so calmly. To them, I wasn't unique – skipper and centre John Bayliss also broke his neck a few years ago and made a successful comeback. 'It's up to you, son,' was just about all that was said.

I owe a great deal to Gloucester. I've had my differences of opinion at Kingsholm on many occasions. But over the years I needed the club far more than it needed me. Young players will always find the going tough until they learn this lesson.

In the end, it doesn't matter who you are. Rugby, above all, is a game where team skill is paramount, especially among the forwards. A casual observer may think that a prop is struggling against his opposite number. But take a close look at what's going on around him before criticizing. Maybe the unit in opposition is operating with greater efficiency.

Back at Cardiff in 1985, therefore, my thoughts were mainly of gratitude for what rugby had given to me. There had been so many tremendous characters in the 1980 Grand Slam side – Fran, Bill, Tony Neary, Roger Uttley, Peter Wheeler and effervescent Steve Smith. Among the Welsh Lions in South Africa I thought of Allan Martin – who christened me 'Phyllis' in honour of his wife – Graham Price, Jeff Squire and Ray Gravell.

After England's game against Rumania at Twickenham during the previous January, I was walking behind the stand when suddenly I felt a tremendous thump on my back. I swung round and there, laughing all over his face, was Irishman John O'Driscoll, another irresistible personality on the Lions' South African venture.

Among Gloucester players, second-row forward John Fidler, crippled by injuries late in his career, showed as much determination as any man I know. When England wheeled him out for one final flourish in South Africa in 1984, he had more bandage wrapped round him than the Invisible Man.

Mickey Burton was the joker of the pack. Yet there was a serious side to him and he taught me a great deal about the technical skills of front row play.

It says much for rugby that the sport does not suffer lasting damage from the sort of isolated explosion of vio-

lence which marred the England-Wales game at Twickenham during the Grand Slam season.

This showpiece occasion, which will be remembered for
the sending off of Welsh flanker Paul Ringer, was not the
dirtiest match I played in. But I am not proud of my
involvement, especially as the game would have been
witnessed in all its gory detail by millions of youngsters
on television.

What must be stressed, however, is that the animosity
of 1980 – brought about, in my view, by Fleet Street's
hype – did not persist much beyond that one day. Any ill
feeling which remained was finally forgotten when players
from both sides found themselves battling shoulder to
shoulder in South Africa a few months later.

Many lasting friendships were forged between English
and Welsh players on that trip and were further cemented
when coach Noel Murphy gathered together a Lions XV
to play Cork Constitution in Ireland during the following
season.

This was a joyful occasion when rugby players were
joined by their wives and girlfriends over one glorious
weekend in a superb hotel. On arrival, we were wined
and dined until midnight when – in typical Irish style –
it was announced that we were all going out! The whole
party descended on the Cork Constitution clubhouse
where the Guinness was still flowing freely at 4 a.m.

But to get back to Cardiff . . . and a memorable day.
Following the lunch, there were cheery exchanges in the
stand with Tony Swift, a fellow England tourist in
Canada, America and South Africa, and British Lions
team-mate Dai Richards. Already, I was rather enjoying
the role of former international.

Out on the pitch, Andrew again underlined his coolness
and class with a gigantic first-minute penalty from
halfway which had the Welsh shaking in their shoes. If
we could just give wings Rory Underwood and Simon
Smith a bit more of the ball, I felt, it might yet be a
famous day for England.

Smith scored a beautiful try in the corner and Swifty
and my immediate neighbour Steve Bainbridge – so ludi-

crously excluded from England selection in 1984–85 by a sending-off in a club game – joined in the celebrations. But sadly these didn't last long.

In the second half, the home pack gained the upper hand in the line-out. Our optimism collapsed when poor Chris Martin at full-back made a terrible mess of a high ball and fly-half Jonathan Davies nipped in for the softest of tries. Wales kept up the pressure and in the end won with a bit to spare.

Even in defeat, however, I felt happy for one England player. When I had told Derek Morgan of my retirement a few days earlier, we discussed the question of a replacement to face the Welsh – no easy matter because England were by no means overflowing with top-class contenders for the loose-head slot.

Several names were mentioned but I had no hesitation in recommending Bristol's Austin Sheppard, who is an undertaker by profession and, as might be expected, finds himself the target of much merriment in a rugby dressing room. He once turned up for an England trial at Twickenham driving his hearse with a coffin in the back. 'Got to pick one up on the way home,' he explained without a flicker of emotion.

'Shep', actually seven months older than myself, is the Charlie Faulkner-type of forward who just seems to go on and on for evermore. He has made more than 400 appearances for Bristol – a fair testimony to any player – but, rather like me, tended to be considered at the top level as purely a tight head.

His one England appearance had been at Cardiff in 1981 when he came on as replacement for injured Fran Cotton – the Lancashire giant's last of thirty-one matches for his country – and I switched to loose head.

Could Sheppard now cope as an international loose head against a Welsh pack which had matched the French in Paris not long before? My opinion was that his selection was justified and I reminded Derek that the Bristolian had been good enough to play in a County Championship final for Gloucestershire in the position some years previously. It would be a considerable advantage that he had been part of the squad all season and knew all the line-out signals and moves. Above all, there was no more dedicated and enthusiastic competitor – before joining the England players in London on the Thursday morning before the trip to Ireland, Shep had insisted on turning out for Bristol on a Wednesday-night game at Aberavon. The hearse covered a few miles that week!

In my judgement, Sheppard passed the test against Wales. All right, England didn't by any means have Jeff Whitefoot, Billy James and Stuart Evans in difficulties, but we were not pushed back in the set and, despite the fact Wales tried several eight-man shunts on our line, didn't lose a head. What more could you ask? My successor recognized the virtue of standing in there square and strong and certainly didn't let England down.

'Meet the challenge,' said Fran. Sheppard did so. And this was the maxim I attempted to follow throughout my career.

2

Bounty Hunter

England's win at Cardiff in 1963 – the last time we managed to beat the Welsh on their own patch – barely registered with me at the time. I had heard of victorious skipper Richard Sharp all right and was making an impression as a thirteen-year-old full-back at a now defunct private boarding establishment called King's School, Sherborne, near Northleach, Gloucestershire.

But rugby was just one of the many sports I enjoyed. I was a country lad brought up in a huntin', shootin' and fishin' environment. I had no great academic aspirations – the only examination I've passed in my life is a driving test – and I longed for the school holidays and a chance to live a life of adventure as a bounty hunter.

I wasn't exactly in the Lee van Cleef mould. But out in the villages around Tewkesbury and Great Malvern the old country traditions still held good and the local farmer could usually be persuaded to part with a small sum if the kids killed a squirrel on his land with an air rifle.

A squirrel's tail would earn a shilling if you were lucky and it was a tanner for a rat. If you shot a magpie or a jay it could be flogged to anglers for fly fishing. But this was small fry compared with one trick which two or three of us lads got up to in my home village of Earl's Croome.

Along at the local church, we used to spend hours with our air rifles trying to shoot down pigeons from the steeple. Once we had bagged a couple, we headed straight to the house of a dear old lady whose favourite meal was pigeon pie. It so happened she was rather blind – just as

22

well because she couldn't tell the difference between the birds we delivered and the wood pigeons which were really what the recipe demanded.

Our reward was half a crown. And that was a small fortune in those days because a tin of 500 air-rifle pellets only cost a couple of bob. The lady seemed quite happy and, presumably, the pigeons tasted all right after a couple of hours in the pot. It can't have done much harm because she lived on for years afterwards!

I'm told that in the dim and distant past the Blakeway family originated in France. It's never struck me until now but perhaps, if things had worked out slightly differently, I might have worn the blue shirt of the home team on my appearances at Parc des Princes!

There's an ancient Blakeway family vault in the church at Chaddesley Corbett, Worcestershire. And it's through rugby that I have learned a great deal more about my ancestry. After my international debut against Ireland in 1980, somebody sent me a very detailed Blakeway family tree dating to William the Conqueror's time. More recently, a lady wrote from South Africa saying that she was descended from Gloucestershire Blakeways who were among the first settlers from this country in Natal. She said her family were so disappointed not to meet me during England's tour of 1984 because 'we have read in the newspapers here that you have a 56-inch chest!'

My grandfather Francis was known as 'Tiny' Blakeway. No one can recall him being lighter than twenty-three stones and he weighed twenty-nine stones on his death soon after the Second World War at the age of forty-nine. He ran a farm at Pamington, near Tewkesbury, but in 1924 also began a fruit-and-vegetable business in Gloucester with another man. One owned the horse and the other the cart. After a while, the partner sold out his share and the present family company of Francis Blakeway Ltd began to prosper.

A great racing man was grandfather. He owned several horses and my father John rode a number of winners for the old man, including the first amateur steeplechase when the Cheltenham Festival resumed after the last war.

One of grandfather's horses was Brains Trust, ridden to victory in the Champion Hurdle by the late Fred Rimell.

Father had been encouraged into showjumping and in 1942 and 1943 competed in gymkhanas alongside one of Britain's most famous riders, Pat Smythe. It was only recently that Pat Smythe succeeded my father as chairman of the British Showjumping Association.

Tiny Blakeway's death occurred just as my father came out of the forces and so he had to decide whether to develop a promising career as a jockey – or concentrate on the family business.

He settled for the latter with the occasional point-to-point ride thrown in. Hunting took a greater part of his life and he subsequently became joint master of the Croome Hounds. He is still very much involved in the sport as joint master of the famous Belvoir Hounds, Leicestershire. It was quite normal for me to participate in the hunt in my younger days.

During those early years, my father sold the Pamington farm and we lived for a while at Kinver in Worcestershire. The fruit business was put in the care of Geoff Butler, who has worked for our family for forty years, and a move was made to a rented farm and country house, Earl's Croome Court. It's a magnificent place where they used to hold the Hunt balls and is now the home of Lord Coventry.

This is where I was brought up, roaming free on the farm and surrounding countryside and also keeping rabbits and pigeons on the top floor and in the attic, where only the kids bothered to go. There's a plaque in the house which commemorates a visit by Judge Jeffreys and the building is also supposed to be haunted – but I can't say that ever bothered me.

I have an older sister Gill, who was in the Great Britain show pony team which defeated America at Madison Square Garden in 1959 and was married to Robert Oliver, a well-known personality in the show world. Gill runs a business producing show horses and also writes for *Horse and Hound* magazine and other similar publications.

There are two younger brothers – Francis and Richard.

We are all directors of a Tewkesbury-based fruit-and-vegetable company, an off-shoot of Francis Blakeway Ltd, and called Threeways Ltd.

It was almost inevitable that I should be a sportsman of some kind. Apart from father's interest, my mother, Joyce, was a county tennis player and qualified for Junior Wimbledon in 1939. Unfortunately, the outbreak of war caused the cancellation of the championships. She was an excellent badminton player too and these days enjoys golf.

All in all, perhaps, not the sort of background which might be expected of a 'donkey' in a Rugby Union front row. I acknowledge I have been extremely fortunate. Many players from very different environments in the north of England and the Welsh valleys have had to make a good deal more sacrifice in pursuit of the same sporting ambition. From the start, my father provided me with the wherewithal to play the game. Unlike numerous international colleagues, my wages were paid when I was absent on tours and it was always possible to take time off when necessary – and for that I owe him a great debt.

The family have followed my career with considerable interest. Even Grandma Fortey, a very gracious Cheltenham lady, liked to know what was going on.

She was seriously ill following a stroke when I made my Twickenham debut in the early 1970s, scoring a try for Gloucester in a fairly rugged encounter against Harlequins. The following day I visited her for the last time before her death and she was still alert enough to produce a newspaper with a report of the game under the headline, 'Wild West Comes to Town'. She was most concerned to know what had happened.

As far back as I can remember, I was steeped in the traditions of the countryside. My first sporting triumphs occurred in local gymkhanas. The achievements were nothing out of the ordinary – strictly the Thelwell-pony type of affair involving sack races and dodging around poles. I often attended point-to-point races with father and he still tells of the day frantic loudspeaker announcements were made because I had gone missing. I wasn't lost – just gathering tadpoles from a pond some distance away.

At about the age of six, I was packed off to boarding school – Wells Court, which is now Bredon School, near Bushley, Worcestershire. Later I graduated to the senior part of the school, Wells House, Malvern, before the move to King's, Sherborne.

I was not a star pupil by any stretch of the imagination. Most of my school hours were spent planning the next birds-nesting expedition or some other hair-raising stunt. What really mattered in those days was escaping with your pals and conquering a tree – in other words, climbing up and up until your head popped out of the top.

We got up to all manner of mischief, invariably operating in a group of three – one to act as look out and the other two to get on with it. I flirted with death one unforgettable day when it was decided we simply had to acquire a heron's egg to add to our collection. The herons, very wisely, had constructed their nest at the top of an enormous pine tree at a spot called Croome Perry. And the intrepid Blakeway was halfway up when the branch below his foot snapped clean off.

I managed to hang on but spent what seemed like hours unable to go either up or down. My one lifeline was a tall thin beech sapling which had sprouted a few feet away and offered the possibility of escape. It took ages to pluck up courage to make a desperate, Tarzan-style leap, grab the beech tree and then spring at ninety miles an hour into a muddy stream below. I was badly winded and soaked through, but otherwise unscathed.

My health was a very serious worry at one stage. I was seven and living at Earl's Croome Court when I suffered severe stomach pains and was rushed into hospital for an operation to relieve torsion of the bowel. My appendix was removed too.

I now know it could easily have been fatal. Admittedly, I had contributed to the situation by riding my sister's large old-fashioned bicycle in defiance of family instructions. A dog chased after me and hit the front wheel, causing the handlebars to fold up and crack into my ribs as I hit the ground. I was very shaken but did not dare admit what had happened until the pain became too much to bear.

Twice more in my life I underwent the same operation. The trouble recurred while I was at Wells Court and the doctors told my father that on no account must I be allowed to play a physical-contact sport again. Fortunately, the advice was ignored. The third time – as I will relate later – came after I had been invalided home from the British Lions' tour of South Africa in 1980.

From start to finish, I hated school and the restrictions it imposed on my outdoor life. I never took the 11-plus due to my operation, but I doubt whether I would have passed unless the examiners had asked questions on wild birds and trees. School seemed to be one long series of detentions, imposed either for something I had failed to do or simply for larking about. There were frequent canings too.

Happiness for me was roaming the woods and fields with an air rifle at the ready. Invariably I was accompanied by my great friend Richard Perry, whose family have been huntsmen for generations.

Even as rather irresponsible youngsters, we applied a code of conduct familiar to country folk. No nest with less than four eggs would be touched and, while sparrows and starlings were fair game at any time, we never shot at songbirds. We fished or whiled away a few hours with Richard's latest pet jackdaw or owl. At one time, he had an owl which used to tap on his bedroom window at night and then drop in to keep him company.

You soon learned not to be squeamish – especially in the flesh house. This was the building near Richard's home – headquarters for the Croome Hounds – which was no more than a glorified knacker's yard. In the countryside, there are always animals which have to be destroyed and, at Croome, there was the occasional race-horse which had been shot. Carcasses arrived in what we called the flesh wagon, the tallow going in one barrel, the bones in another and the meat being cooked to be fed to the hounds. They even brought in an enormous boar one day.

The place stank. But we didn't give it a thought. Inside, you could find the juiciest of maggots – just right for the next morning's fishing trip on the Croome river.

On other days, we hunted rats. Farm buildings were a good bet. If that failed, a chicken carcass could be placed on the farm's brick heap and we just lay in wait. Often, we missed the target and the crafty vermin would eventually get wise to our game and refuse to return. But with the bounty running at a tanner for each victim, it was well worth persisting.

You had to be careful with rats, they were dangerous things if the hunter ventured too close. But other creatures could be even more dodgy. One of our favourite games, when life seemed a little tedious, was Bait the Bull; this involved jumping into the pen and seeing how angry the animal became before we made ourselves scarce. We must have been crazy. I saw a bull flatten a wall one day.

School, as I have indicated, was one long bore. Anyone who says that this is the best time of his life must lead a very dull existence indeed.

I couldn't wait to escape Sherborne – because I had far more important things on my mind. My only real ambition was to see if I could carve out a career as a full-time sportsman.

Wells House and Sherborne had at least brought out a certain talent as a 100- and 200-metres runner (I was fastest in my age group). My strength had enabled me to produce a fairly quick time over a couple of lengths of the swimming pool and I could ride a pony and fire a rifle. Now if I learned to handle a sword as well there was a fair chance I could make a name for myself . . . in Modern Pentathlon.

In the mid-sixties, Britain's Modern Pentathlon Association began to despair of ever succeeding in any competition with the eastern-bloc countries. The sport here was mainly confined to the Services and, while excellent all-rounders were produced who could excel at most of the disciplines, no one seemed to be able to ride a horse.

Eventually, somebody decided to go to the Pony Club of Great Britain to see if they could unearth any likely lads who might be able to run and swim to a reasonable standard as well as ride. What a bright idea it was! Quite apart from the fact that I was to devote much of the next three years to the sport and reach a fair standard, the approach led to the discovery of Danny Nightingale, a Somerset lad whose only sporting interests until then had revolved around the local gymkhana scene.

Danny, of course, was to help put the sport well and truly on the map eleven years later when he, Jim Fox and Adrian Parker took on the rest of the world at the Montreal Olympics and carried off the team gold medal.

I left Sherborne School with only one idea in mind – to reach the top as a Modern Pentathlete. Father soon introduced me to the fruit-and-vegetable business. This wasn't a career I had thought long and hard about; I just went off to work with him in the car each morning and a new life developed from there.

Luckily, father was quite content for me to pursue this new interest. I swam in the mornings and shifted a few fruit boxes before setting out on a lunch-time run. Then, after another brief work appearance in the afternoon, I strived with increasing dedication to improve my riding or learn the new skill of fencing.

The man who was to have the greatest influence on my development in the sport was Gloucester scrap-metal merchant Robbie Phelps, already well established in the British Modern Pentathlon team. His career featured four Olympic Games and he is coach to the present British team which includes his nephew, Richard. In 1984, Robbie was awarded the OBE for his services to the sport – and no accolade was more richly deserved.

In those early days, I often trained with Robbie – or rather attempted to keep up with him. He was a patient tutor but what rubbed off on me more than anything was his phenomenal self-discipline and commitment. It was something which benefited me enormously when eventually I decided that rugby offered a more exciting future.

Robbie needed all the determination he could muster. Modern Pentathlon, as I have indicated, was traditionally a Services activity – and normally restricted to the upper echelons. For an outsider – especially a scrap-metal merchant – to break in and gain acceptance was in itself an achievement. I soon gained an idea of the extent to which it had been a sport for the privileged few – you had to be invited to competitions, which were invariably at Service establishments, and mind your p's and q's.

A significant Phelps move was to form Britain's first civilian Modern Pentathlon Club – the Spartans, of Gloucester. I was one of the youngest and most enthusiastic members, increasing my training all the time and even varying the routine on one occasion by running home after work – a total of sixteen miles. The experiment wasn't repeated.

To be honest, I doubt whether I could ever have made it to the very top. I was fine on the track over 100 and 200 metres. But the longer distances weren't for me. I would have struggled at the very highest level as a swimmer as well.

At fifteen, however, I was all set to be a world-beater. If Robbie said you could go quicker, you did. He was that sort of bloke. Fencing was difficult at first. Another of the original Spartans, Mike Thomas, taught me the rudiments of the sport and spent hour after hour cussing me.

Still, the achievements of Robbie, Mike and others in establishing Modern Pentathlon in Gloucester were remarkable. Facilities at the time were woeful – certainly nothing to compare with the Service establishments. But these lads had the burning ambition to overcome almost any obstacle.

By 1968, I fancied my chances at the British Under-21 Championships held at Croydon. This involved all five disciplines – running, fencing, shooting, swimming and riding. I finished third with Danny Nightingale trailing some way behind in ninth place. What effort he must have put into the sport in the years which followed!

My performance earned me selection as reserve for the World Junior Championship in Aldershot that year – but this was to be the peak of my Modern Pentathlon career.

There was no cut-off point when I simply decided that enough was enough. It was more a question of rugby posing an irresistible new challenge. Much to Robbie's disappointment, I had been playing for Cheltenham Colts for some time. 'You want to forget that silly game,' he told me one day. 'You might get injured.' Not a bad judgement, I suppose.

Until my introduction to Cheltenham, rugby had meant little more than a welcome break from the class-room. I was never a forward then. As I had a bit of pace, enjoyed tackling and relished the prospect of catching the ball and charging hell for leather at the other boys, I was invariably at full-back. It helped being fairly beefy for my age. Obviously I threw my weight around a little bit too much as far as the teachers were concerned because, at Wells House, I was stopped from playing with my classmates and told to join the bigger lads.

No one actually spotted my potential as a rugby player although, on leaving, a member of staff fixed me up with a game or two for a Clifton Vacation XV at the club's former ground in Eastfield Road, Bristol.

Cheltenham introduced me to the delights of the front row and very soon I was serving an apprenticeship as a loose-head prop – always my position with that club. Although I was obviously very fit from all the activity since leaving school, it was clear that rugby required something extra.

I began weight training and circuits, also doing press-ups and sit-ups. By now, I was working harder for Francis Blakeway Ltd as well – and that was good for building even more strength because, at the time, it involved humping boxes and crates all over the place. As I was doing less running and swimming and also eating bigger meals, my weight increased – from the thirteen stones of

31

the Modern Pentathlete to the sixteen-and-a-half stones which was the level I retained throughout my international career.

Although the Modern Pentathlon dream had disappeared, the influence of the dedicated Robbie Phelps remained. He and Fran Cotton would have got on like a house on fire. As Fran used to say, 'If you've talent in the first place, think how much more you can make of yourself through sheer hard graft.'

Very soon, I was making the occasional Cheltenham first-team appearance; and only recently somebody handed me a programme of a match in 1970 when we played Rosslyn Park at Roehampton. It makes fascinating reading because I note that, in those days, you could buy a Park season ticket for £2 and it cost four shillings for ground admission, plus another four shillings for the grandstand. Even more interesting were the teams on that day. Cheltenham had a useful side, including county threequarters John Berry and Bob White, fly-half Bob Redwood and hooker David Protherough.

Phil Keith-Roach, who was brought up in Cheltenham and educated there, was in the home line-up, offering a reminder of just how durable some first-class front-row forwards can be. Keith-Roach had knocked around in the Bristol United side in the early 1960s and went on to captain Rosslyn Park for years. He was still going strong until 1984 when neck trouble finally forced him to call it a day.

The Rosslyn Park pack also featured another forward who seemed to go on for ever – Andy Ripley. I was to play with 'Rippers' on many occasions in future years. And what an amazing character he is! Whatever the match, he seemed to introduce an element of humour – and was always at his best in the occasional Sunday or mid-week fun game.

I shall always retain vivid memories of playing for Mickey Steele-Bodger's XV against Cambridge University at Grange Road very late in my career. Ripley was skipper for the day and determined to make the most of it. Our powerful side included several All Blacks, obviously

proud to be chosen and suitably keyed up for the game.
Imagine their shock, therefore, when the captain stood
up in the dressing-room and said, 'Now, let's start by
introducing one another – first name only and birth sign.'
The roll call around the dressing-room duly took place
with the puzzled New Zealanders beginning to wonder,
'Who the hell is this guy?' It was only the start because
Ripley's pep talk was brief and to the point. He merely
blew on his fingertips, rubbed his hands together enthusi-
astically and said, 'Well, this is it boys. Everybody do his
own thing.'

There was just one instruction – on how to operate a
short penalty move. The plan was to huddle together and
then mutter a terrifying Maori-type war chant which went
something like 'Azza, azza, azza' (a gentle leg-pull aimed
at the grim-faced All Blacks). Then we would whip the
ball out for New Zealand wing Craig Green to score.

When the big moment came, it didn't quite work as
intended because Green was clattered to the ground by
half a dozen students. Ripley was determined not to be
thwarted. Another tapped penalty opportunity came
along and we were instructed to gather in a group and
then scatter in all directions, leaving Green with the ball
and a clear run into the corner.

Again, something went wrong. Poor Green was buried
once more. As the winger staggered to his feet, I said,
'Hey, Craig, Rippers has just worked out a third one for
you.'

Green was not amused. 'You can bloody well forget it,'
he drawled. 'I've had enough. Is the guy crackers?'

All the fun and games meant that by half-time we were
struggling to beat a useful-looking University side. 'Well
boys, we had better do something about it,' the skipper
suggested laconically. And we did. Ripley could still play
very seriously when he had to and was never anything
but a wholly committed tackler and runner. More of the
big man later.

My move to Gloucester, the reasons for which I shall
explain in due course, came not long after the Rosslyn

Park game. My debut was against Moseley on a day when all the first-team players were absent on county duty.

Establishing myself at Kingsholm was bound to be a long job. Mike Burton and Robin Cowling were the first-choice props and Keith Richardson was the United loose head. Richardson subsequently became club captain and pushed out Cowling, who hardly suffered as a result. He moved on to Leicester and won eight caps between 1977 and 1979.

By 1973, however, I had been given a number of senior outings at tight head when Burton was absent on international duty. My first big representative break came that year as well . . . a place in the England under-23s side against Japan at Twickenham.

The game was won 19–10 and it is interesting now to reflect what a valuable breeding ground this proved for the senior international team. Dusty Hare kicked the goals and there were two more players destined to appear in the 1980 Grand Slam side – scrum-half Steve Smith and flanker Mike Rafter. Bob Wilkinson, capped for the first time in Australia two years later, was in the second row with Peter Warfield (already making his mark in the senior side) at centre, Peter Squires on the wing and Neil Bennett at fly-half. Our hooker was Northampton's Jon Raphael, so unlucky to sit on the bench for England nineteen times and never win a cap.

I didn't quite complete the game because of a knee injury which was to be a considerable frustration for several weeks afterwards. I paid 25 guineas to a specialist in London who told me it was a cartilage problem. Later, a second opinion suggested I had damaged knee ligaments. 'Keep going as long as you can,' I was advised. I did and, despite the odd niggle, the knee survived the next twelve years of rugby.

After this brief flirtation with the England scene, it was back to Kingsholm to add a harder edge to my game. At that time, the Gloucester lads still tended to regard me as a seven-a-side star as much as anything else – something which might surprise people who watched my international matches some years later. When I arrived at

Gloucester, however, I still had my schoolboy sprinting ability and was rated the quickest forward in the club.

We took sevens very seriously for a while and I used to start off as one of the three forwards but immediately switch to the wing. The idea was that I should use my pace and power to bludgeon a way through the opposition. It was surprisingly effective.

My career continued steadily throughout the 1974–75 season. Then, quite out of the blue, I was picked for the England senior tour of Australia. At last, I thought, the big breakthrough.

3

Bash-a-Pom-a-Day

To describe England's 1975 tour as eventful is the biggest understatement of all time. Quite apart from the fact we were kicked and punched from one end of Australia to the other, I witnessed Gloucester team-mate Mike Burton make history by becoming the first Englishman to be sent off in an international. I landed in deep trouble myself and at one stage was due to be sent home in disgrace on the next plane.

Subsequently, I had the extraordinary experience of appearing for England in a match where an unmistakable stench of booze wafted up from our front row. To cap it all, I was branded a thug by the Rugby Union president and told I would never represent my country again. Quite a start to my senior international career!

It wasn't as though there had not been considerable controversy before we flew from London in May. Bristol forward David Rollitt, who was on the trip, grumbled for years afterwards that England 'sent boys to do a man's job'. This, to a great extent, was true because, out of a twenty-five strong party, no fewer than twelve of us were new to this level of rugby. Seasoned players like fly-half Alan Old, scrum-half Jan Webster, full-back Peter Rossborough, prop Barry Nelmes, lock Chris Ralston and back rows Peter Dixon and John Watkins had all been left behind. To make matters worse, men such as Fran Cotton and Peter Preece were injured early on and a total of five replacements had to be flown out – centre Jeremy Janion, Alan Old, scrum-half Ian Orum, Dixon and Nelmes.

The selection which caused most comment was that of young flanker Steve Callum, of Upper Clapton, who had appeared from nowhere (as far as most of us were concerned) on the strength of an England schools' tour of Australia the previous year and a couple of county games.

In some respects, I counted myself very lucky to be selected. At Gloucester, I was by no means a first-team regular and there were many accomplished props who could reasonably have expected to get in ahead of me. Unlike Callum, however, I had been through the mill, playing for Cheltenham and Gloucester in Wales on numerous occasions. I believe I got the vote ahead of Colin Smart because it was recognized I could operate on both sides of the scrum.

Callum, through no fault of his own, was out of his depth. And he wasn't the only member of that tour party who hasn't been heard of since. Alan Wordsworth, for instance, who played in the first of the two Tests when Neil Bennett was carted off, showed himself to be an extremely talented fly-half – but he wasn't ready for the hurly burly of this trip.

This was the England party which began the tour:

Backs: P. E. Butler (Gloucester), A. J. Hignell (Cambridge University), P. J. Squires (Harrogate), A. J. Morley (Bristol), D. M. Wyatt (Bedford), P. S. Preece (Coventry), K. Smith (Roundhay), A. W. Maxwell (New Brighton), W. N. Bennett (Bedford), A. J. Wordsworth (Cambridge University), W. B. Ashton (Orrell), P. Kingston (Gloucester).

Forwards: F. E. Cotton (Coventry), M. A. Burton (Gloucester), P. J. Blakeway (Gloucester), J. V. Pullin (Bristol), J. A. G. D. Raphael (Northampton), W. B. Beaumont (Fylde), R. M. Wilkinson (Bedford), N. D. Mantell (Rosslyn Park), R. M. Uttley (Gosforth), A. G. Ripley (Rosslyn Park), D. M. Rollitt (Bristol), A. Neary (Broughton Park) capt., S. R. Callum (Upper Clapton).

Alec Lewis, the genial former England flanker from Bath, was tour manager with the thoughtful John Burgess, so successful in the north at the time, as coach.

Before we left, Lewis said, 'We have chosen a large number of uncapped players, not because we think there will be easy pickings in Australia, but because this seemed an opportune time for us to begin our rebuilding.'

How wrong could he be? The Wallabies had been mauled in England and Wales two years earlier and were determined to improve. Ray Williams, of the Welsh Rugby Union, went out at one stage to help establish a national coaching system. Dave Brockhoff was appointed national team coach – and, in my view, this is the man who must shoulder much of the responsibility for what took place.

The Wallabies were simply over-motivated by the time the new-look England side arrived. To start with, there's nothing an Australian likes better than to beat an Englishman. And clearly they had decided that the best way to rugby success was by intimidation and physical means.

At one time, the British Lions were bitterly criticized for their famous '99 call' – the signal for every forward to lay into the opposition. The 1975 Australian version was 'putting the biff on'. I couldn't make it out when this happened early in the tour. Normally, it takes an incident of some kind to spark violence – but in this case there was no reason. It was to occur time and again and the attitude of the Australian people and press hardly eased the tension. A radio station at one venue ran a 'Bash-a-Pom-a-Day' feature. The slogan was visible everywhere on car stickers.

No one anticipated so much aggravation and controversy as the tour approached. I was thrilled to be picked and think that I was viewed for the first time as an up-and-coming international player. I did not expect to make the Test side – Cotton, John Pullin and Burton were likely to play. But I was determined to impress as much as possible and, as the only other prop in the party, there was always a chance that an injury to Cotton or Burton would lead to a cap.

It was comforting that there were so many West Countrymen on the trip. Peter Butler, Alan Morley, Peter

Kingston, Burton, Pullin and Rollitt were all established Gloucestershire players. I was also to get to know the promising new second row forward from Fylde – W. B. Beaumont.

A brief fuel stop in Calcutta certainly opened my eyes to the ways of the world. I was only a country lad from Tewkesbury after all. 'Leave the plane if you wish, but it is advisable not to do so,' said the pilot. So naturally we did. We were also told, 'Don't drink or eat anything. If you must have a drink, make sure it is from a sealed container and that you don't let this touch your lips. Just pour it in.' Imagine my shock when the doors opened and dozens of Indians appeared and proceeded to spray disinfectant everywhere, just in case we brought disease into Calcutta!

Burton was my first room-mate in Australia. We just couldn't shake off the effects of jet-lag and sat up at four o'clock one morning writing postcards home.

But there was no time to be lost before adjusting to the rigours of rugby. I was picked for the first game against Western Australia at Perth – an easy start because there isn't a great deal of Rugby Union in that part of the world. We romped to a 64–3 win and I felt that I had performed satisfactorily – although I could hardly fail to do so with Pullin and Cotton alongside me in the front row.

It was quite a day for Morley, who grabbed four tries, and Neil Bennett, who amassed 36 points from two tries, three penalties, eight conversions and a dropped goal. That was just one point short of Alan Old's world record with the British Lions the previous year. 'I could have beaten it if I had realized how close I was,' said Bennett later.

The powder keg exploded three days later. I was replacement for the match with a far more powerful Sydney side ... our first meeting with the Phantom Puncher.

Steve Finnane is a barrister and a very nice man – off the field. On it, he is nothing but trouble and earned his nickname through his diabolical antics during this tour.

Finnane was the man appointed to soften up the Poms and he struck when least expected – invariably when the referee's back was turned some forty or fifty yards away.

One of his tricks was to turn as you moved from one situation to another and then deliver a vicious blow. If you were running at a fair pace, the combination of momentum and the punch could have dire consequences. He whacked Bill Beaumont in this game and put him off for stitches.

Another troublemaker was flanker Ray Price, subsequently to excel in Rugby League. His habit was to feign injury and then, as play moved close to him again, jump to his feet and leap into the fray – invariably hitting someone in a white shirt in the process.

He late-tackled Wordsworth in that game – far later than the challenge which led to Paul Ringer's famous sending-off for Wales against England five years later. Wordsworth was stunned and sat there with an expression which said, 'I've come here to play rugby, not for all this.'

Finnane thumped young Callum in the Sydney game as well and we were beaten 14–10. By far the biggest blow, however, was the loss of our forward lynchpin Fran Cotton with a pinched sciatic nerve. I replaced him near the end and he took no further part in the tour.

It is no coincidence that Finnane never embarked on a major tour. He knew what would happen to him. Unfortunately, the Australians were still countenancing his behaviour in 1978 when Finnane broke Graham Price's jaw in two places during the Test against Wales in Sydney. I was interested to read subsequently that Price didn't rate Finnane highly as a player and described him as someone who 'sought vindication behind feeble chauvinism'.

The events I witnessed at Sydney angered me, so much so that it led to me dropping one of the biggest clangers of my career.

At the time, of course, I was young and green. I had not yet experienced dealing with the rugby journalists of Fleet Street – let alone Australian reporters who didn't even tell you who they were.

The England players had finished training and were relaxing with an orange juice or two round our Sydney hotel pool when I fell into casual conversation with these characters. They began chatting about the violence of the previous Saturday and stupidly I fell for the bait and opened my big mouth.

'Where I come from,' I boasted, 'we might lose the game but we don't lose the fights.' And I added, 'If somebody wants to start it, we'll carry it on. It's not difficult to get involved and doesn't necessarily require great strength – my grandmother can hit you with a baseball bat and do plenty of damage.'

To add fuel to the fire, two or three of the England lads began larking about and I was soon flexing my muscles and adopting a Mr Universe pose – with a camera clicking away all the time.

Imagine my horror when the pictures and my comments – totally ill advised in the tense aftermath of the Sydney defeat – were splashed all over the newspapers, both in Australia and then England.

I was summoned to John Burgess's room where the tour management gave me a right dressing-down. There was every likelihood, they said, that I would be sent home on the first available flight. I was also to be dropped for the next match – although the Australians later persuaded England not to take this course.

My apologies did little at first to calm a serious international incident. Yes, I told Alec Lewis, I said those things, but my words had been used out of context to make a sensational story. Also, I stressed, I had been conned and hadn't the faintest notion I was talking to journalists.

Eventually, the management must have recognized my naivety and decided on a reprieve because, by the following Saturday, I was in action at Sydney Sports Ground against New South Wales – and Mr Finnane.

For once, the Phantom Puncher kept his fists to himself. Centre Peter Preece had a wonderful match, scoring four tries, and we lifted morale again with a 29–24 win.

I learned a great deal from the Sydney hotel affair.

Even now, my responses to questions from pressmen will often be brief and to the point. Some you can trust; certain others, you can't.

Rugby tourists are always likely to be a target. In my innocence, I had been set up and there have been occasions since Australia when I have seen it coming and stepped in very firmly to prevent serious trouble. It happened on the Lions' South African tour in 1980 when a group of pretty, scantily dressed girls suddenly turned up around an hotel pool and the cameras appeared. We very soon put a stop to that.

No matter how careful you are, however, trouble can still arise. While touring with England in South Africa in 1984, a newspaper came out with a totally fictitious story that I had punched coach Dick Greenwood. Everyone knew it was rubbish – but by the time other pressmen had had their go, it very soon became fact in the minds of the readers.

There was still a price to pay for the muscle-man story. In normal circumstances I might well have replaced Fran and won a first cap in the opening Test, which was to follow only one week after the New South Wales match. England, however, had called for Barry Nelmes, the former Bristol forward who had moved to Cardiff, as Fran's replacement. I am convinced that at the time I was a better player than Nelmes. But the management must have decided that, in the light of all the bad publicity, it was too much of a risk to include me in a Test.

To my great disappointment, Nelmes had one warm-up game and went straight into the international. From then on, the tour became more and more of a let-down as far as I was concerned.

The fourth game took us to Goulbourn, a small, dusty town with one main street. It wouldn't have surprised me in the least to see Wyatt Earp ride through. A New South Wales Country XV provided the opposition at the Workers Arena and it was fairly obvious their forwards were picked to soften up England a bit more before the first Test.

42

In every respect, this was another disaster for the tourists. Before the game, we learned that Peter Preece would not be fit for the Sydney international because of shoulder trouble. And in the first half, fly-half Bennett went off with a back injury – a problem which was to recur.

Once again, I was a replacement and, despite heavy-handed tactics from the home side, the England pack played reasonably well. But wing Derek Wyatt missed a good chance and, although he did score on another occasion, we lost 14–13.

What hope for England in the first Test? Not much, I'm afraid. The original unwise selection policy of experiment was already in tatters and Alec Lewis, John Burgess and Tony Neary thought long and hard before naming a side.

There were five new caps. Gloucester's record points' scorer Peter Butler was at full-back; Andy Maxwell in the centre; another Gloucester player Peter Kingston at scrum-half; Neil Mantell, then of Rosslyn Park, in the second row; and, of course, Nelmes.

Inevitably, Finnane and his pals put the biff on and there was an almighty punch-up early on. Bennett, still not fully recovered from his back injury, had to be replaced after fifteen minutes by Wordsworth. Worse followed when skipper Neary was forced off in the twenty-third minute with a knee problem, finishing his tour.

Australia won 16–9 in front of a 40,000 crowd, with Mark Loane, already on his way to becoming one of his country's most capped players, scoring their only try. Not for the first time, we were bitterly critical of an Australian referee – in this case, Billy Cooney. The day after the match, the management sent another cable for the experienced Lions, Old and Dixon, to join us.

John Pullin, no stranger to the job, took over the captaincy but there was still only a seat on the replacements' bench for me in the sixth match against Queensland at the new Ballymore ground, Brisbane. Nelmes was now firmly established ahead of me.

Queensland was not expected to be a pushover, especially as it had beaten the great Lions side of 1971 in the opening match of that tour. For once, however, England found reasonable form and triumphed 29–3, scoring tries through Janion, Ripley, Morley – a centre replacement after twenty minutes for the injured Maxwell – Bob Wilkinson and Peter Squires. Young full-back Alastair Hignell impressed sufficiently to displace Butler and win his first cap in the second Test and there were excellent performances by Morley, one of the successes of the trip, and no. 8, Ripley.

The second Test followed four days later, also at Bally-more Park. We wondered whether the bash-a-pom policy could possibly continue. Our dressing room after the international in Sydney gave the impression that World War III had just taken place. White shirts tend to show every speck of blood.

What seemed so crazy was that the Australians possessed players of considerable skill. Skipper John Hipwell, as he proved in England, was a world-class scrum-half with a beautiful pass. The backs were all strong and direct, Garrick Fay proved a tower of strength in the middle of the line-out and Loane and Price were quick, mobile and good with their hands.

Sadly, there was to be no let-up in the violence – the second Test was one of the most sickening spectacles in international rugby history. Firstly, however, England had to pick a side and, apart from choosing Hignell, Bedford lock Wilkinson also made his debut. Preece was fit enough to partner Janion in the centre and Old brought extra steadiness at fly-half. But there was no room for Dixon. Poor Dixon. He was to travel 20,000 miles to miss a cap and play just one game at the end of the tour.

Another ironic twist was that big Fran was still with us and fully fit – but denied a chance to return because England had already committed themselves to Nelmes. After the second game, in Sydney, I had watched Cotton crawl in agony across the floor on all fours to reach the toilet and there seemed no chance he could consider playing rugby for weeks.

Manipulation from an osteopath sorted him out, however, and he would dearly love to have mixed it with

Blakeway, the fruit and veg man! This photograph was taken at Gloucester Market on the day I was selected for a senior England debut against Ireland in 1980

Wearing the Barbarians' shirt – a proud moment for any rugby player

All eight England forwards are visible in this remarkable picture taken during the narrow win over Scotland in 1985. Gary Pearce and Steve Brain complete the front row, with Wade Dooley and John Orwin sneaking a crafty look from behind. The back-row trio are John Hall (No.6), Bob Hesford and David Cooke

Two ways to jump a fence. I was a member of the Croome Hunt Pony Club team which came second in the British Junior Pentathlon Championships in 1966

The start of my international career – England Under-23s face Japan at Twickenham in 1973

I could not have been more fortunate to launch my international career in such experienced company. Pictured from left to right during the Irish game at Twickenham are Roger Uttley, myself, Peter Wheeler, Fran Cotton and Tony Neary

Steve Finnane (left), the Australian prop who was at the centre of so much controversy during the England tour of 1975. We called him the Phantom Puncher

Exit Paul Ringer (right). Irish referee David Burnett orders off the Welsh flanker at Twickenham. England fly half John Horton wonders if his jaw is still in one piece

Mike Burton, my Gloucester team-mate, became the first England player to be ordered from the international rugby field during the infamous Battle of Brisbane

Finnane and company. But there was nothing the management could do because they were tied by the International Board tour agreement. A similar fate befell Ray McLoughlin, the Irish prop, in New Zealand in 1971.

Like me – the perennial replacement – Cotton prepared to watch the infamous Battle of Brisbane.

The pictures do not convey the full horror of the cold-blooded violence dished out by the Australians in the name of rugby. There were no preliminaries. I watched in amazement at the kick-off as the home forwards went berserk with boot and fist. Barry Nelmes, the first to gather the ball, lay on the ground, shaking his head from right to left in a desperate attempt to save himself from being kicked unconscious.

I often look at a photograph which shows Andy Ripley standing back, hands on hips, and surveying the carnage. A hard man is Ripley. But this, it was clear, was not his idea of fun.

England had been critical of referee Bob Burnett, of Queensland, in the previous game. Now we fumed because he failed to take a grip and issue a final warning through the captains. Loose-head prop Stuart Macdougall and one or two more Australians could well have been sent off during those early bitter exchanges. They were definitely greater sinners than Michael Alan Burton, who carved himself an unenviable place in the rugby history books with his fourth-minute dismissal.

Burton's crime was a late tackle on winger Osborne after a clearance kick. Certainly it was a bad foul. And it's true that England's prop had been spoken to previously for a butting incident. But in the light of all that had taken place, the decision was ridiculous.

England, of course, had no real chance after that – especially as Burnett still failed to curb the Australian violence. RFU president Ken Chapman, once a Harlequin forward, described the match as 'a disaster for rugby football' and I wouldn't disagree.

What can be said is that the seven remaining English forwards fought a tremendous rearguard action, with Bill

45

Beaumont, the emergency prop, revealing the character which was to surface time and again in future seasons as England captain. England actually led 15–9 at the interval thanks to some superlative goal-kicking by Old, who landed one penalty from inside his own half. There was also a fine try by Squires.

Inevitably, the tide turned in the second half. Two tries in a ten-minute spell by young fly-half Wright – Australia's outstanding back in the two Tests – put his side 17–15 ahead and very soon the lead increased to 30–15. Only a late Roger Uttley try, the result of a typical swashbuckling run by Ripley, brought respectability to a final score line of 30–21.

What scenes there were afterwards. The English dressing room was full of long faces. Outside, there was already frantic diplomatic activity and a meeting was soon underway downstairs.

Burton was on the carpet. Exactly what was said, I don't know. But my Gloucester team-mate was left in no doubt that he had disgraced the name of English rugby by his actions. Undoubtedly, there was a certain amount of sympathy for him – only reasonable in view of what had happened – but the management still felt he had overstepped the mark. The following day, he was given an official caution by a disciplinary committee – and that was the only punishment meted out.

Of far more concern to the Australians was the attitude of the angry English officials, who were ready to cancel the Australian tour of our country in 1975–76. Once we had arrived home, Ken Chapman issued this press statement:

After the violence in the early stages of the match, I got together with the next president of the RFU, Tarn Bainbridge, and tour manager and chairman of selectors Alec Lewis. We agreed that we should inform the Australian authorities that if their illegally aggressive approach were maintained in England we should not want them there. We told them that there would be sendings-off and all sorts of trouble, which we were not prepared to tolerate.

Fortunately, the Australian authorities seemed as disturbed as us and assured us that they would take steps to put their house in order. However, until we can be assured that we shall not be confronted by the same over-aggressive approach as we experienced during the last month, the English section of the winter tour remains in jeopardy.

These words emphasise the gravity of the situation. Burton, normally the tour's court jester, said all the right things in public. 'I was fairly sent off. I was warned once and over-stepped the mark, but the laws were inconsistently applied and others could have been dismissed.'

Privately, he was distraught. His world had caved in. Although he might joke about the incident now, 'Burto' was only too well aware of the shame he had brought upon himself as the first man in more than a century of English rugby to be ordered off. Deep down, he felt an intense pride in representing his country.

Surprisingly, perhaps, the after-match dinner passed without any great incident. Rugby players are extraordinarily forgiving folk the world over and, despite all the viciousness on the field, there were the usual handshakes afterwards.

But the tour wasn't over yet for either Burton or myself. From the warmth of Brisbane we moved to the Sports Reserve, Townsville – a little spot in the middle of nowhere – for one more game against a Queensland Country XV.

Incredibly, the hit-a-pom attitude still applied, although first there was a chance to take a boat to a delightful place called Paradise Island just off the coast and enjoy a barbecue.

Originally, I was due to play tight head with Nelmes on the loose. But by then, I suspect, the Cardiff giant had had enough. He cried off, explaining that he was feeling the effects of a knee injury and so Burton, who had escaped a ban, returned to the fray with me as loose head.

What the tour management had not fully compre-
hended, however, was that Burton, determined to drown
his sorrows, had spent the interval between the second
Test and the Townsville trip on the most monumental
bender of all time. Yet still he played. When he took the
field, he would have flopped a breathalyser test by a
considerable margin. In fact, England's tight head was
extremely tight.

The home team must have caught a whiff of the booze,
although their only interest was in inflicting grievous
bodily harm on anyone wearing a white shirt. To add to
the pressures, it was a night game in steaming heat – and
in one crazy moment all the tensions of the previous weeks
caught up with me.

The flashpoint came when scrum-half Peter Kingston,
my club-mate from Gloucester, dive-passed following a
line-out and was then set upon by a thug who literally
trod on his head. I saw red and immediately ran up and
hit Kingston's assailant. He didn't go down – so I
whacked him again and again. A little while after he quit
the game, suffering from concussion.

The match itself was straightforward enough, although
why we were ever asked to take on this extra fixture I
will never know. Alan Morley was again in sparkling form
with two tries. Dixon managed some action too. But there
was no doubting the highlight – a try by the inebriated
tight-head prop.

It was the only one Burton scored throughout his
England career and the mixture of elation and alcohol led
to the sort of scene you would expect after a last-minute
FA Cup Final winner at Wembley. He charged halfway
round the pitch offering the crowd a celebratory double-
fisted salute.

The humour of this moment and the relief of a 42–6
win was soon forgotten in the tin hut beneath the stand
which was our changing room. Ken Chapman walked in
bristling with anger and, within the hearing of all the
other players, told me I had brought fresh disgrace on
English rugby. 'You will never play rugby for England
again,' he stormed.

This onslaught, regarded as quite out of order by the other England lads, should have worried me. But at the time I could not have cared less what happened in the future. I did not see why we should spend weeks touring a country, soaking up formidable punishment, and not exact some form of revenge.

We flew home the next morning and I was mightily relieved to be out of it. I had started in Perth full of enthusiasm and optimism, but little had been achieved from my point of view.

It was true that I had gained important experience as a member of a senior tour for the first time and, despite the RFU president's castigation, had reasonable prospects of making further progress. But somehow, due to a combination of odd selection and injuries, the party never quite gelled into a team. The chemistry wasn't right. And, of course, I had not won a precious first cap.

Despite all the problems, there are still a few happy memories of the tour. I made lasting friendships and met some superb characters. But the Australians detested the Poms and J.P.A.G. Janion seemed to sum up all that they imagined of the average Englishman.

A perpetual pipe smoker, Jeremy Janion, the centre replacement for Keith Smith, played for Richmond and wore a cravat to match his rather posh public-school accent. He was a delightful man with a tough competitive edge and, despite his late arrival, emerged as one of the personalities of the trip.

Then, inevitably, there was 'Rippers'. What a man! In recent years, Andy Ripley has made quite a name for himself as a television celebrity and author of an unusual and original book called *Ripley's Rugby Rubbish*. This strange volume is subtitled, The Essential Ego and Massage Book, which in itself sums up the bloke.

Ripley was already very much the individualist back in 1975. Swapping shirts with an opponent after an international is standard practice. But exchanging tour blazers is another matter altogether. Our giant back-row forward did this with Wallabies hooker Peter Horton – the smallest man on the field – following the Sydney Test.

This threw Alec Lewis into a dreadful panic. Who would have Lewis's job with men like Ripley around?

Earlier, Ripley had been put in charge of a training stint in Perth. There was a running track adjoining the stadium where we played and, as a top-quality athlete, this was right up his street.

Our temporary coach fancied a few 400-metres dashes – not exactly my cup of tea. But he approached the session in typical laid-back fashion. 'If you want to do it boys, you can,' he said slowly. 'If it doesn't suit, fair enough. Do as you feel.' Somehow, we all battled through some extremely competitive one-lap dashes.

I enjoyed the widely varying Australian country and climate and wish now that I had made more of an opportunity to do some sightseeing. On my return, I vowed that if future travel chances arose I would take full advantage.

Much later, an England tour took me to Canada and America where the players – in keeping with rugby's macho image – were determined not to view 'tons of water falling onto a load of rocks'. Personally, I enjoyed Niagara Falls.

Australia also offered an opportunity to meet one of the numerous Blakeways who emigrated from Gloucestershire and settled there. Uncle Roger, a clergyman, thought nothing of driving several hundred miles to spend a few minutes chatting to me in Perth.

The Aussies are sports mad. In Sydney, I watched Rugby League, Rugby Union, hockey, lacrosse, Australian-rules football, soccer, golf and athletics take place during the same day on one small area adjoining our hotel. Nearby, tennis courts were open from six o'clock in the morning until late at night.

Our tour may have been a disappointment in a rugby sense. But the hospitality was warm and the food magnificent. I devoured steak almost every day for seven weeks. When I arrived home, Ros had gone to great pains to prepare me a very special meal. Naturally, it was steak!

4

Disaster . . . and Triumph

Tries by P. J. Blakeway are something of a collector's item. I managed just one for Gloucestershire in the County Championship – and did it with a broken neck.

Since the ill-fated adventure Down Under, I had knuckled down again to club rugby, gradually edging up the front-row pecking-order at Kingsholm. In the early days after my move from Cheltenham, I was sixth choice out of six and mere cannon fodder for the likes of Mickey Burton. But by the start of the 1977 season I was bursting with energy and soon celebrating a County Championship debut against Devon at Gloucester – we won a fairly uneventful game 20–6 – and then appearing in a win over arch-rivals Somerset at Bridgwater.

Disaster day was Wednesday, 26 October. Gloucester had a home match that night against South Wales Police who, at the time, was a shadow of the side which can now give any club in the land a run for its money. We won, as expected, but at one point I found myself trapped at the bottom of a ruck, receiving a fearful crack on the back of the neck.

It was a pure accident and provided me with quite a jolt, but wasn't bad enough to prevent me finishing the game. In any case, I wasn't keen to admit any problem because Gloucestershire was due to play the South-West Championship decider against Cornwall at Camborne that weekend. I managed to keep out of trouble when the Gloucestershire lads trained at the Cleve club in Bristol on the Thursday evening and kidded myself that some gentle massage of the neck from the sympathetic Ros had eased a nagging pain.

Unfortunately, there had been no magic cure. The game was only just under way at Camborne when the Gloucestershire forwards got up a fierce head of steam and went for a pushover try. The Cornish scrum disintegrated like a pack of cards and I felt an agonizing pain which certainly got no better as the game wore on.

'Get your head up, get your head up,' pleaded hooker John Pullin, as we went down for another scrum. 'I can't, I can't,' I groaned. Even claiming that precious try and winning 35–13 brought no real joy and, by the time I lurched into the showers, I could not even wash my hair. I just stood with my back to the wall and let the water run over me.

This was just the start of a nightmare. I had travelled independently to Cornwall at the last minute because of work commitments and so, having made my excuses for opting out of the after-match reception, faced a 230-miles drive home. Luckily, I had the company of two teammates from the Gloucester club – fly-half ChrisWilliams, capped once by England, and centre Richard Mogg. 'Keep a look out over your right shoulder and tell me if anything's coming,' I told Chris. If the road was clear, I signalled and pulled out to overtake . . . and we were still using the same, precarious method of navigation when at last the lights of Gloucester came into view eight hours later.

I went to bed but found the pain unbearable. Eventually I turned to Ros and muttered, 'Get me to the vet.' She was three weeks away from giving birth to Laura, and a right pair we must have looked as we shuffled into Gloucester Royal Hospital. The staff rushed out with *two* wheelchairs!

The X-rays revealed a broken vertebra; only the muscles developed from front-row play had kept the bone in place and averted potential disaster.

They stuck me in traction, a very painful experience. It made my jaw ache and ache and, worst of all, my 'gravity-feed system' wouldn't operate – in other words,

I couldn't spend a penny! Eventually, I had to wait for
Ros to come in and draw the curtains so that I could
whip off the awful neck contraption and do the business.
How I longed for that wonderful visiting hour!

Finally, the doctors realized what I was up to and
exchanged my medieval jousting outfit for a plastic jacket
and helmet, which I wore for three-and-a-half months.

Blakeway was finished as a rugby player. That, at least,
is what everyone assumed until the night I returned to
Kingsholm to watch a real battle of the heavyweights –
Gloucester *v.* Pontypool.

I slipped in at the back of the stand, still in my
supporting collar. And there sitting nearby was Terry
Hopson, puffing away thoughtfully on his pipe. Terry is
held in high regard at Kingsholm. He was a magnificent
fly-half for both club and county and might have reached
the top but for the fact that he broke a leg in the same
place twice against the same opposition. He's a shrewd
man too, speaking slowly and deliberately in a monotone.

'Well,' he observed, puffing hard on the pipe, 'you only
need to get in four games for England. Then (another
puff) you would go with the British Lions to South Africa.
After that (further lengthy pause) you could retire,
couldn't you?'

I laughed dismissively, but somehow his remarks stuck
in my mind. It was to be a very long time before I
reminded him of his prophesy. He hadn't forgotten. 'I've
never told a soul . . . and never predicted a thing in my
life before or since,' he chuckled.

It was to be eighteen long months before I ventured
onto a rugby field once more. 'There's no reason why you
shouldn't play,' Ray Davies assured me. 'The big question
is whether you can overcome the mental barrier of facing
the physical challenge of rugby.'

There was hardly time to give that side of it much
thought. I had negotiated just two matches for Gloucester
United and two more for the first team when, quite out
of the blue, England – beaten 10–9 by New Zealand a
few weeks previously in a grinding forward struggle at
Twickenham – summoned me to the final international

trial. The date was 5 January 1980, and Blakeway was in dreamland.

Originally, I was picked in the same Rest XV as my Gloucester pals Gordon Sargent and Steve Mills, a comforting thought. But there were so many withdrawals that, when we took the field, my two mates had been promoted to the opposition. In fact, only two of the nominated Rest forwards actually appeared – 'Nasty' Nigel Horton (a nickname he acquired from playing too much French club rugby) and myself.

The England XV won easily enough by 28–10 and, to be honest, I didn't perform that well. Judging by his press coverage before the match, it seemed that Clint MacGregor, the Jamaican-born Saracens tight head, only had to turn up to clinch his first cap.

Imagine my surprise, therefore, when that wily old Gloucester sports' journalist Arthur Russell – sadly, no longer with us – telephoned me on Sunday night and said, 'I'm 99 per cent sure you're in. I got it from London.'

'You're having me on,' I said. 'The team won't be known yet. Thanks all the same for the call but . . . goodnight.'

Arthur was right. It shows how naive I was at the time because the following morning I set off in the fruit-and-veg wagon and called in at the local newsagents at 6 a.m. for a paper, not realizing that the RFU always make team announcements at 10.30 a.m. on Mondays. But I was *in*. The impossible had happened. Two years and three months after breaking my neck I was to win a first cap against Ireland at Twickenham.

There was little time for celebrations. In those days, England had just established the system of Monday evening get-togethers at Stourbridge – infinitely better than a Sunday drag – and I was astonished when about 2500 people turned up to watch our practice.

Naturally, I was dashing everywhere, eager to impress. At that point, the huge figure of loose-head prop Fran Cotton edged towards me and, in his deep Lancastrian voice, boomed, 'What the hell are you doing?'

'I'm trying to get involved,' I replied nonchalantly.

'Look,' he said patiently, 'all you have got to do is *stand in scrum, stand in line-out.* Anything else is pure bonus.'

Those words will stick in my mind forever. Fran and the likes of Bill Beaumont, Roger Uttley, Tony Neary, Steve Smith, John Carleton and Mike Slemen had already achieved so much with Lancashire and the North, figuring in the All Blacks' only tour defeat at Otley not long before. They knew just what they wanted. I was the new boy and, in Fran's words, had only to 'jog along'. 'Stand in scrum, stand in line-out and keep out of the way,' he repeated. 'Everything will be OK.' And how right he was.

Winning the Grand Slam – England's first since 1957 – Triple Crown and International Championship didn't enter my head as the debut against Ireland approached. And I reckon chairman of selectors Budge Rogers and his colleagues must have written us off on the spot when, during practice at Bisham Abbey, Gordon Sargent popped me through a scrum as clean as a whistle.

Sarge is a fair operator. His career began at the Lydney club in the Forest of Dean, where they breed 'em tough. Gordon was in the Gloucestershire colts' side at fifteen – and he had his piratical bushy black beard then.

There was no way that the Old Forester was going to cause me serious problems, however, unless something was wrong. Obviously, Budge looked furious. 'Don't worry,' I assured him. 'All I have to do is adjust the position of my arse.' And, quite literally, that's all it was.

The point was that for the first time I was privileged to be propping in front of William Blackledge Beaumont, the man who was to prove such a fantastic inspiration to every member of England's all-conquering side. I have never met a second-row forward who pushed so hard, whether it was in training, practice games or an international. He was so powerful that I had to make crucial adjustments in technique to cope with it – and it was while we were sorting this out that Budge saw me heading skyward. It was never likely to happen again.

The big day passed in the blinking of an eye. Everything, it seemed, happened at ninety miles an hour. At one stage, we were 9–3 down and Ollie Campbell was kicking everything. But Bill kept us going, Dusty Hare matched Campbell's accuracy with the boot, and by half-time tries by Steve Smith and Mike Slemen had put us 15–9 ahead.

Tragedy struck in the second half when Sale centre Tony Bond broke a leg and had to be replaced by Clive Woodward. Towards the end, however, John Scott went from a scrum ten metres out for our third try and England had won 24–9.

It's interesting to record the teams in that first international of an historic season. England was to rely on only nineteen players throughout the tournament, Maurice Colclough (injured for the Ireland game) returning for Nigel Horton, Paul Dodge succeeding injured Nick Preston and Mike Rafter operating as replacement in one game for Roger Uttley. For once, England showed some consistency in selection and this was an important factor in our success.

Ireland bristled with talent. I confronted Phil Orr; in fact, the forwards were very largely the Dad's Army pack who were to achieve long-awaited Triple Crown glory for their country two years later. These were the sides:

England: W. H. Hare (Leicester), J. Carleton (Orrell), A. M. Bond (Sale), N. J. Preston (Richmond), M. A. C. Slemen (Liverpool), J. P. Horton (Bath), S. J. Smith (Sale), F. E. Cotton (Sale), P. J. Wheeler (Leicester), P. J. Blakeway (Gloucester), N. E. Horton (Moseley), W. B. Beaumont (Fylde) capt., R. M. Uttley (Wasps), J. P. Scott (Cardiff), A. Neary (Broughton Park). Replacement: C. R. Woodward (Leicester) for Bond, sixty-one minutes.

Ireland: K. A. O'Brien (Broughton Park), T. J. Kennedy (St Mary's College), A. R. McKibbin (London Irish), P. P. McNaughton (Greystones), A. C. McLennan (Wanderers), S. O. Campbell (Old Belvedere), C. S. Patterson (Instonians), P. A. Orr (Old Wesley), C. F. Fitzgerald (St Mary's College), G. A. J. McLoughlin (Shannon), M. I. Keane (Lansdown), J. J. Glennon (Skerries), J. B. O'Driscoll (London Irish), W. P. Duggan

(Blackrock College), J. F. Slattery (Blackrock College) capt. Replacement: I. J. Burns (Wanderers) for McNaughton, thirty-three minutes. Referee: Corris Thomas (Wales).

Overall, I didn't think I performed that brilliantly in my first international. But we did nick one against the head late on and, subsequently, the press seemed to feel I had done well – and, naturally, I always believe what I read in the newspapers!

England selectors were obviously happy to leave well alone. In that one match, after all, we had scored more points than England managed in the whole of the 1979 championship. So, two weeks later, we were off to Paris, only too well aware that England hadn't won there for sixteen years.

The 1964 side included back-row forward Peter Ford, the old Gloucester greyhound. He still does a great job behind the scenes at Kingsholm and, typically, his advice to me was brief and to the point, 'Just get amongst them and they'll be rattled. Once they start talking a bit, you will know they can be beaten.'

Jean-Pierre Rives and his lads were certainly yapping quite a lot when we wiped out an early 7–3 deficit and led 17–7 thanks to tries by Preston and Carleton, plus two sweet little dropped goals from John Horton, the will-o'-the-wisp fly-half from Bath.

It was not the most gentlemanly of games. Early on, a French forward trod on Roger Uttley's head, putting him off for a while with a gash which looked as if it had been inflicted by a butcher's knife.

But this was the match when I really came into my own at international level – mainly due to a crazy piece of selection by the French. Salas was an enormous fellow. But the man from Narbonne was definitely a natural second-row forward and not a loose-head prop – and I had a high old time sorting him out.

While Fran coped with Paparemborde – one of the great tight heads of my era – I was able to burrow underneath the bulky Salas and cause all manner of disruption to the French scrum. Again, of course, Uncle Bill offered maximum support.

The match would have been perfect but for the fact that I was the victim of another act of thuggery near the end and suffered the rib injury which, much later on, was to have such disastrous consequences in South Africa. I was trying to do Bill Beaumont a favour at the time. The skipper was trapped on the floor and it was obvious that if I didn't get across and block the path of some sinister-looking French forwards, he would be well and truly clobbered. In making my move, I was put to ground and can then remember this figure closing on me. I swung round to protect my head – and got booted in the ribs.

When trainer Don Gatherer arrived with the magic sponge I could hardly breathe. But I was determined to stay on because France was battling to save the game. There was a glorious mixture of relief and utter elation when the ball was kicked dead for the last time and we had won 17–13.

The beano which followed can rarely have been matched in the long history of international rugby. The dressing room resembled a casualty clearing station at the Battle of the Somme . . . but no one worried too much. We lay in the huge bath which was deep enough for the water to come up to our necks and I remember champagne bottles and empty cans bobbing on the surface towards me. By 5.30 p.m. I was sufficiently anaesthetized not to bother too much about my extremely sore ribs.

The Grand Slam had suddenly become more than just a dream, although we didn't give it much thought at the time. A lot of the lads had suffered heavy defeats in Paris before and also experienced other setbacks with struggling English teams of the 1970s. Now, the frustrations and disappointments of the past were buried. This was to be party time for Bill and the boys.

It was many hours later that I staggered up to bed. Room-mate Dusty Hare was already in residence, quite dead to the world but still clad in evening dress, which is traditional attire at after-match dinners. I took off my jacket, undid my trousers, lost balance . . . and fell in a heap on the floor. Neither Dusty nor myself had moved a muscle when Paul Dodge discovered us the next morning.

I felt dreadful. My head was thumping, ribs throbbing and the rest of my body protesting as well. At least I remembered to collect the oysters – a gift from the French which, in a more sober moment, I had left in the care of the hotel staff. Whatever happened, I was going to carry those back to Gloucestershire as a present for my wife.

I arrived home in a terrible state, walking sideways up the stairs to ease my painful ribs but still clutching the precious oysters. 'I'm not eating those,' said Ros. 'They could be off.'

5

Twickenham's Blackest Day

The match against Wales at Twickenham followed two weeks later and was to bring a day of shame for British sport and an unwanted place in the rugby history books for Llanelli flanker Paul Ringer. Could England slay the Red Dragon for only the second time in seventeen years? The players certainly thought so, although my main concern as the game approached was that troublesome rib.

England physio Don Gatherer looked serious as he carried out his examination and I could actually hear a clicking sound from the rib cage. 'What's up?' I asked nervously. Don hesitated and then muttered something about 'crepitation'.

'Come on,' I snapped. 'Don't give me that smart-ass talk. What does it mean?'

'I reckon you've broken a rib,' he said and promptly despatched me to Westminster Hospital. Don, I learned many weeks later, was spot on with his diagnosis. But, much to my relief at that time, the X-rays failed to pick it up and it was assumed I had ripped a cartilage. With the help of a pain-killing injection, I was able to scrummage with reasonable comfort . . . effectively enough, it was agreed, for me to face the might of Wales.

It's doubtful whether the rugby mecca of Twickenham has ever been the venue for such a brutal game. From the moment full-back Dusty Hare fielded a high ball and was cruelly kneed in the back, it was all-out warfare.

Bill Beaumont and Maurice Colclough slugged it out with their rival locks Geoff Wheel and Allan Martin;

Ringer charged around like an enraged bull and soon the boots and fists were flying everywhere. I admit I played a full part in the mayhem. But what do you do? When team-mates are being punched and trampled on, there's no point in standing around and letting it happen. Englishmen may have a reputation for being a bit soft. But they're not like that down Gloucester way and, if it meant fighting for survival, I was ready.

What had caused such an explosion? In the first place, I blame the press for going way over the top in their build-up of the match. One article I read ranted and raved about the English being responsible for shutting down the pits and steel works and suggested that this was the opportunity for Welsh revenge.

What a crazy notion! It doesn't need such rubbish to encourage every player to be totally fired up in an international between England and Wales. The occasion is enough.

It was soon very clear that the match was in danger of going beyond the control of Irish referee David Burnett. He called Bill and Welsh skipper Jeff Squire together to issue a general warning, but this had little effect – especially in the case of Ringer.

Fourteen minutes had elapsed when he committed a crude, late tackle on fly-half John Horton. In normal circumstances, it would have merited nothing more than a ticking off and a penalty. But the warning had been given and, to retain any sort of credibility, Mr Burnett had no alternative but to order him off.

To an extent, I felt sorry for Ringer. I knew from his days with Leicester that he had rather a hot temper. A few years later, he was ordered to an early bath again while playing Rugby League with Cardiff Blue Dragons – for thumping one of his own team! On the other hand, I hate to see any player dismissed in an international because this brings such disgrace on himself, his family and his country.

Ringer, it must be remembered, was the first man to be sent off in an international at Twickenham since New Zealander Cyril Brownlie – fifty-five years earlier. The

man from Llanelli was hounded by press and public afterwards and it was months before he could resume anything
like a normal existence.

The match, as I have indicated, represented everything
that is bad in rugby. It just festered into an ugly boil,
with poor Roger Uttley in the wars once again when
Welsh boots performed a tap-dance on his head and
inflicted another horrible injury which forced him off.
Bristol's Mike Rafter – rightly described as Rafter the
Grafter for his ball-winning skills – took over at half-time.

Wales, in my view, was stupid to get itself embroiled
in aggro because it was a talented side and could well
have beaten us and wrecked those title dreams. As it was,
the seven-man Welsh pack really raised its game and we
were staring defeat in the face when wing Elgan Rees
rounded off a typically adventurous run by hooker Alan
Phillips to steal an 8–6 lead.

Even with fourteen men, Wales had outscored us 2–0
on tries. And they would have won if good old Dusty had
not come to the rescue. What a cool customer he is!
Having kicked two penalties and missed a few more, he
was offered one last chance in injury time from way out
on the right touch-line. I couldn't watch, but a deafening
roar confirmed he had done it and to chants of 'England,
England, England' we left the field in triumph.

Every Grand Slam side needs a certain amount of luck.
We had snatched our share for the season in one crazy
afternoon of bloody tribal conflict.

And so to Murrayfield and an occasion when rugby's
image was restored in a Calcutta Cup match of glittering
quality. After our great escape at Twickenham, we
couldn't wait to get at the Scots and finish the job in
style. And I was convinced we could do it – providing,
that is, my ribs caused no further bother.

It's a good job that drug-testing wasn't common practice in sport in those days because I would have failed
dismally. Quite apart from having another pain-filling jab
– a further X-ray at Gloucester Royal Hospital again
failed to pinpoint the fracture – I had been given a fairly
potent concoction by Gloucester Rugby Club doctor Tom

Durkin. It had got me through a club game without too much pain a few days earlier. So I took an extra gulp before facing Scotland – not something I would recommend because I was as high as a kite!

What a start we had! We shoved the Scottish forwards all over the place and applied the wheel to disrupt their put-in. A couple of ghosting breaks by that elegant centre Clive Woodward created tries for wings John Carleton and Mike Slemen and, with only half an hour gone, England was 16–0 up.

It was a remarkable performance against a handy Scottish side. I always remember forwards rather than the dancing men of the backs when I reminisce about my big games and I have good reason to think of the rival loose head on this occasion – because Jim Burnett, of Heriots FP, had also made a comeback to rugby after breaking a bone in his neck.

Then there was Alan 'Timber' Tomes, the huge Hawick lock, who did his best to deprive Carleton of one of the three tries he scored that afternoon. At one point, we lined up a pushover in the corner and turned it into the most devastating scrum I was involved in throughout my career. We sank low and then . . . whoomf. With Big Bill shoving for all he was worth, Scotland would have been catapulted straight onto the terracing if the crafty Tomes hadn't dropped it in the second row. We went straight over the top of him and Steve Smith grabbed the ball to put Carleton clear on the blind side. What a shunt! Later, Scotland played a full part in a brilliant attacking spectacle. Even 'Timber' – the Great White Man – sneaked a try as an England lead of 23–6 with barely twenty minutes left was drastically reduced.

Then, disaster struck. Roger Uttley wrestled the ball from a ruck and thrust his elbow into my rib cage. In darts terminology, he had hit the bull – smack on that very tender spot which had caused me so much discomfort. I was creased. I couldn't speak when Don Gatherer arrived on the scene and resigned myself to going off.

Enter Fran Cotton, a man who is big in body and big

63

in heart. He stuck out a Desperate Dan chin, grabbed my collar and said very slowly, 'You don't leave this field when we are ten minutes from history. You're staying.'

No one argues with Cotton. I stayed. In a fever pitch of excitement, the Orrell Express completed his hat-trick – the first by an England player since 1924 – and England had won 30–18.

Bill Beaumont was carried shoulder high from the field and Tony Neary, now the most capped England player, led the champagne celebrations. It was an incredibly emotional affair, especially because so many of the side had known times when a Grand Slam and Triple Crown seemed a million miles away.

There had been a revolving door in the 1970s through which player after player was propelled at a rate of knots by the England selectors. Most of the triumphant team of 1980 had international experience – but not together. Neary, for instance, was good enough to captain the British Lions in a Test in New Zealand in 1977 and yet he couldn't make the England side in the following season.

At last, however, England had got the mixture right. Whether this was through shrewd judgement or sheer good luck, I'm not sure. All I knew in this moment of ecstasy was that my rib hurt like hell – but nothing was going to stop me joining another riotous party.

Whatever they say about the Scots being tight with money just isn't true. I got involved with a bunch of them that night – and we drank our way through a small fortune. It must have been the booze which resulted in my leaving behind a posh dress-shirt when we began the journey home the following morning. A few days later, a package arrived at my home and – initially, at least – I was delighted to discover the missing item. Then a note dropped to the floor. It read, 'Here's your shirt, I've laundered it, love Sue.' Try explaining that one to the wife!

'Get your passport ready,' said Roger Uttley. 'And don't forget the sunglasses. You're going to South Africa.'

A Lions' tour? It was a possibility, I agreed. But surely this *Boys' Own* story could not go on forever? I was still quite bewildered by the speed of it all, pinching myself to realize that just over three months before I had been playing for Gloucester United in the wilds of Wales, desperately hoping I could regain full fitness and perhaps recapture a first-team spot by the end of the season.

I had made the England side on the strength of just five matches – two for Gloucester United, two for the senior-club side and an international trial. I had even become a Barbarian – and figured in a County Championship final as well. It was almost too much to take in.

What made the England side of 1980 such a potent force? Firstly, no praise is high enough for Bill Beaumont. Purely as a second-row forward, England has not subsequently produced anyone of his calibre. He played his rugby as he lives his life – dead straight. He went in hard and fair every time, hurling himself into situations where many a strong man would flinch, sadly, I suspect, causing the damage which eventually put him out of the game.

A mighty player was Bill. But he was also man enough and astute enough to recognize that people like Fran, Nero, Peter Wheeler and Steve Smith had a lot to offer. Bill was the guv'nor, all right. But we were all encouraged to say our piece – and a great feeling of comradeship and will to win developed in this way.

Another crucial ingredient of the side was experience. The pack included three past captains – Cotton, Neary and Uttley. Like Bill, incidentally, all had been born in Lancashire. Later, of course, John Scott and Peter Wheeler as well as scrum-half Steve Smith and centre Paul Dodge took a turn in charge. That's eight skippers in all, a quite remarkable statistic.

In general, therefore, there was a great wealth of talent and know-how in the ranks. From hooker Wheeler, a true competitor, I learned a great deal. Maurice Colclough – known as Fez – was another marvellous servant of England, who operated in the middle of the line-out

65

during the Grand Slam but moved to the front with equal effectiveness two years later when Bill retired. That might not sound a particularly difficult transition, but the demands of the two jobs are very different – especially at international level.

Behind the scrum, I always admired the skills of Mike Slemen. Not only was he a winger of the highest class but he also operated as a type of auxiliary full-back, taking the touch kicks when they were on Dusty Hare's wrong foot. Slem was a true footballer with an innate sense of where to be at a particular time. Even as a front-row donkey, I fully appreciated his contribution.

There were many times as well when we valued Dusty's assistance. The Nottinghamshire farmer was Mr Reliable himself. He suffered more 'drops' by England than I've had retirements – and that's saying something. But every side needs a decent goal-kicker and we had the best. Certainly, the Welsh team of 1980 won't dispute that assessment.

As you will now realize, Fran Cotton has had quite an impact on my career. In fact, he seems to have been on hand at almost every turn.

His efforts on behalf of England in Grand Slam year were immense. I had learned to respect him as a player and a person as far back as 1972 when I attended an England under-23 get-together at Lilleshall and found myself packing down against the England senior forwards who were preparing for the tour of New Zealand.

Fran was my opponent and I remember feeling a certain amount of trepidation at the thought of taking on this mountain of a man. He ground me into the turf; it was just as well we were practising and not playing a full-scale match because I might not have survived the experience.

We met again some months later in a club fixture. I had just made a comeback, after another of my injuries, by playing in a game which opened the clubhouse at local junior outfit, Coney Hill. I was immediately picked for Gloucester against Coventry at Coundon Road and Fran lined up in a home front row which also featured hooker

John Gallaher and that rugged old England forward Keith Fairbrother. There is no love lost in Gloucester-Coventry clashes and this was no exception. We were beaten – but I had coped far more satisfactorily against Fran and felt very encouraged. Despite his bulk, Fran was a superb sevens player – not the sort of rugby relished by too many prop forwards. He played at tight and loose head, not only for England but for the British Lions as well – and this was at a time when there were many fine specialists vying for both positions. It's true that I was also selected on both sides of the scrum for England – but I became a loose head in the final season only because there was no one else around.

When the flak was flying, Fran could look after himself as well. Like myself, he came from a part of the country where they don't stand any messing about.

We often roomed together on England trips. 'King Kip' I called him, because he liked a lot of sleep. That suited me – you're often up with the lark in my line of business and I was invariably ready to catch up with a bit of shut-eye. That 1980 trip to Scotland was something special from that point of view. Through a stroke of good luck, a friend of Fran's wife was responsible for room bookings at the superb, five-star Peebles hotel which was our weekend headquarters. We could hardly believe our eyes on being shown to a room which was bigger than my house. Fran and I had been given a luxury suite with balcony and breathtaking views of the beautiful border country. Each bed was big enough to take three Cottons. And placed delicately on each pillow were two roses. 'Eh up,' said Fran. 'Somebody fancies us.'

Fran has always been very helpful to me. In 1975, for instance, we were together with the England party in London before flying out to Australia. Naturally, as the new boy, I had everything – spare toothbrush, toothpaste, shoe polish and reserve shoe laces.

He showed me his bag. Apart from official tour kit, it included one mouldy jockstrap and a very dubious-looking towel. That was all. 'How on earth will you manage?' I asked. 'Look,' he said. 'Everything is provided. Send what you want to the laundry in the morning and it'll be back all neat and tidy at night. You need a track suit, tour kit and a pair of jeans – no more.'

That, indeed, was how Fran survived. Mike Burton was even better. He wore shorts and an Adidas tee-shirt which he never took off during the whole tour. I'm certain the shirt walked around without him in the end.

Fran and I went through many adventures together. We were also arch rivals in the glorious 1980 season because the County Championship final between Lancashire and Gloucestershire was squeezed in during the international programme. I hadn't played for Gloucestershire since the never-to-be-forgotten Cornish escapade. But they brought me back to face Fran, Steve Smith, Bill Beaumont, Tony Neary, John Carleton and Mike Slemen at the picturesque Vale of Lune ground, where there were pigs roaming among the spectators on a grassy bank and it absolutely belted with rain.

It didn't altogether surprise me that we lost 21–15. Lancashire was on the crest of a wave at the time. They had played together all season and, in addition to the England boys, the side contained Irish international full-back Kevin O'Brien – a match-winner on the day with two tries – and solid characters like centre Tony Wright, lock Jim Syddall and flanker Roger Creed. Fran, incidentally, was at tight head and took on Gordon Sargent.

Gloucestershire, by comparison, was ill prepared. Because of the busy representative and club season, we hadn't managed a single training session together in the three-month gap since the semi-final – and it showed. When we called a short penalty move, we all moved one way and the ball went the other.

The county selectors at Gloucestershire have a reputation for making distinctly controversial choices on the big occasions and this match was no exception. Alastair Hignell, capped fourteen times by England at full-back between 1975 and 1979, was picked at centre. Hignell had never played a serious match there in his life and, although he possessed sufficient footballing ability to make a fair job of it, this was hardly the ideal time for experiment. We fought hard to stay in the match but, in the end, Lancashire's superior team-work paid dividends and Bill Beaumont collected the trophy.

6

Life with the Lions

Terry Hopson's crystal-gazing in the grim days when I
was trussed up in a neck brace had been accurate to the
very last detail. Two days after the great Murrayfield
celebration, I was one of eight Englishmen named in the
thirty-strong British Lions' party for the tour of South
Africa. There would have been more players but for the
fact that neither Tony Neary nor Roger Uttley was able
to travel.

The rib was still a big worry. If it continued to niggle,
I thought naively, I could always have another pain-
killing jab. Whatever happened, it was not going to stop
me catching that plane. This was my Olympics. The
chance might never arise again.

Irishman Syd Millar was the tour manager with
another highly respected former Irish international
forward Noel Murphy as coach. Bill Beaumont was
captain – who else? – and this is the party which set off
with high hopes of success on 3 May 1980:

Backs: B. H. Hay (Scotland), R. C. O'Donnell
(Ireland), J. Carleton (England), H. E. Rees (Wales), M.
A. C. Slemen (England), P. Morgan (Wales), R. W. R.
Gravell (Wales), J. M. Renwick (Scotland), D. S. Rich-
ards (Wales), C. R. Woodward (England), S. O.
Campbell (Ireland), W. G. Davies (Wales), T. D. Holmes
(Wales), C. S. Patterson (Ireland).

Forwards: P. J. Blakeway (England), G. Price (Wales),
F. E. Cotton (England), C. Williams (Wales), A. J. Phil-
lips (Wales), P. J. Wheeler (England), W. B. Beaumont
(England) capt., M. J. Colclough (England), A. J. Martin

(Wales), A. J. Tomes (Scotland), S. M. Lane (Wales), J. B. O'Driscoll (Ireland), J. Squire (Wales), C. C. Tucker (Ireland), J. R. Beattie (Scotland), D. L. Quinnell (Wales).

The tour, of course, was a disaster as far as injuries were concerned. Rodney O'Donnell, Mike Slemen, David Richards, Gareth Davies, Terry Holmes, Fran Cotton, Stuart Lane and myself all returned home early for various reasons. The replacements were Andy Irvine (Scotland), Paul Dodge (England), Tony Ward (Ireland), John Robbie (Ireland), Ian Stephens (Wales), Phil Orr (Ireland) and Gareth Williams (Wales).

Right from the start, things began to go wrong. Instead of a week's preparation in Eastbourne, which had been standard practice for Lions' parties of the past, we were whisked straight out to a training camp at Vander-bijlpark, not far from Johannesburg. In theory, it wasn't a bad idea – especially as there were plenty of groups back in Britain anxious to voice their opposition to anything connected with South Africa. The trouble was that we were on the high veld, some 6000 feet above sea level. You need time to acclimatize – and the management didn't give us a chance.

Murphy, one of the few non-drinking Irishmen I know, immediately proposed a 'light work-out' although all of us were still feeling the effects of a twenty-four hour journey. In reality, he proceeded to run the living daylights out of us. Even the fittest boys – let alone the little fat lads like me – were poleaxed. I recall Allan Martin, the Panther from Aberavon, taking off in a sprint round the athletics track, which made him extremely unpopular with the rest of his struggling colleagues. But we were soon chuckling because, on the second time round, we discovered him spreadeagled on the ground gasping for breath.

Very soon, we were training for three hours morning and afternoon. In that heat and at that altitude, it was a suicidal policy. It knocked the stuffing out of us before the first game was played and I am sure took its toll in the Tests. We all had new boots to start the tour but, inevitably, these led to blisters on the hard grounds and many of us continued to train somewhat painfully in socks.

Murphy actually succeeded in crocking Ollie Campbell, one of the fittest men I know. The Irish wizard tweaked a hamstring and this was to cause him a great deal of aggravation later on. If we had worked flat out every morning for perhaps three hours, nobody could have grumbled. But flogging it in the afternoon as well was too much. It was meant well, but killed people off.

Before leaving for South Africa, Mike Burton had warned me to expect a rough ride. 'Every training scrum will be like playing in an international,' he said.

Burton was right. The point is that there are no passengers on the Lions tour. You have two full sides of the highest quality and there is formidable competition for places. It's one thing pulling on a Lions shirt for the first time but another matter altogether winning a place in the Test side, which is every player's goal.

The forwards were very soon laying into each other at Vanderbijlpark. The sessions were often frightening in their intensity. I soon found myself up against Fran and, in one particularly fierce, no-holds-barred session, our long-standing friendship was set aside.

In fact, I would go as far as to say that this was the moment when, in effect, the tour was wrecked for both of us. I did him up . . . and he did me.

At the time, I was lined up with Welsh hooker Alan Phillips and loose-head prop Clive Williams against Fran, Peter Wheeler and Graham Price. If Pricey dropped a scrum, I dropped the next one. Bodies smacked into one another. And when we did take a break, the coach had us running in all directions. 'Run here, run there,' shouted Murphy. At night, those words frequently recurred in my dreams.

Murphy would never allow a player to rest with his hands on his knees. 'Stand upright,' he yelled at me on one occasion. 'I am standing upright,' I replied, causing considerable mirth among the rest of the lads. By now, Fran was definitely feeling the strain – I was too –

although no one could have imagined that within a couple of weeks he would be admitted to the intensive-care unit of the Grootte Schuur Hospital, Cape Town, suffering from a suspected heart attack.

My ribs, never right from the start, were complaining too. And my tour prospects plummeted shortly afterwards when we arrived at Port Elizabeth for the first match against Eastern Province. During the hurly burly of another practice, a scrum half-wheeled and I battled for all I was worth as the shunt continued. Suddenly, I felt a dull pain and collapsed in a heap – Fran's shoulder had caught me on that tender spot once again.

For a while I did my best to make light of the problem, hoping against hope that it would go away. I could not stand straight in the morning and soon got into the habit of rising at 6 a.m., staggering to the hotel jacuzzi and sitting there while the jets of water played soothingly on my chest for a couple of hours. John O'Driscoll, the Ireland back-row forward and a doctor in London, found me there one morning and was appalled. 'You've been there for two hours? Ten or fifteen minutes is supposed to be maximum. Any more than that will drain all your strength away,' he said.

Clearly, I was fighting a losing battle. But at least I did manage one appearance for the Lions. This was the second fixture of the tour in East London against the multi-racial South African Rugby Association's Invitation XV, known as the Leopards.

Inevitably, I received another crack on the ribs – fortunately in the late stages. As we were well on the way to a fairly comfortable 28–6 win, I opted to go off. The management had made it clear that this was a long tour and, with plenty of reserves available, there was no point in staying on unnecessarily and aggravating an injury. Fran wasn't too pleased because he had the job of replacement prop and it was so near the end that he had removed his boots. He got a ticking off for that.

It was agreed there was little point in doing much about my injury until the Lions had moved on to Durban for the next fixture against Natal. Eventually, I went to the medical centre there for the inevitable X-rays and sat numbed as the doctor said to me, 'You have broken a rib. And it didn't happen here.'

He showed me the evidence. The X-ray picture revealed quite clearly a crack with a callous on top which had separated from the bone. 'If you had left it alone and rested, it would have healed on its own,' said the doctor. 'but it has parted somewhere along the line. It's reckoned to be medically impossible to have a broken rib for eight weeks – but somehow, you've done it.'

As if I hadn't received a big enough shock, there was more to come. Because the healing process had not followed a normal course, the hospital authorities were worried that gangrene might set in. So I was moved on for exhaustive blood tests, all of which proved negative. To say the least, I was very relieved.

In my heart, I knew the tour was over. This was confirmed subsequently when Bill Beaumont took me to a meeting with Syd Millar – I had jokingly labelled him Syd Vicious during one particularly arduous training stint – and Noel Murphy. They were very fair, saying that I could either go home or take a brief rest and then see whether I was able to survive an all-out fitness test against the other Lions' props.

Had I been single without any particular responsibilities in England, I would probably have opted for the latter. But I had left Ros at home with a young daughter, a son of six weeks and a house to run. There was always the risk I could get cracked yet again and this time the bone might penetrate my lung, causing very serious problems. 'I'll go,' I said sadly.

At least I wasn't the most short-lived Lions tourist of all time. Poor Stuart Lane, the Welsh flanker, had lasted less than a minute of a first match in which Eastern Province was beaten 28–16. Without an opponent in view, he stepped into a dip in the pitch and made such a mess of his knee that he was immediately counted out.

Before returning home, there were a few enjoyable days as a spectator. The fourth game against a South African Rugby Federation XV at Stellenbosch was no picnic, however. The main object of the Federation front five seemed to be to soften up our forwards before the first Test. But the Lions were in no mood to be mucked about. Fran had been involved in a rugged duel with a hefty character called Hennie du Toit when suddenly he walked from the field clutching his chest. His third Lions' tour had come to a sad and premature end.

Everyone was profoundly shocked after the match to hear than Fran was apparently in a very bad way. Thankfully, however, there had been no heart attack – the problem was subsequently diagnosed as a condition called pericarditus, an accumulation of fluid in the muscles of the heart, and Fran made a full recovery. I shall relate more of this incident later on.

I remained in South Africa long enough to see the Lions go down 26–22 in a thrilling opening Test at Newlands, Cape Town, on 31 May. The Springboks had learned a lot from the hammering they received from the 1974 Lions and were no longer kicking away good possession. They had an extremely solid pack and a running back division with a fly-half in Naas Botha who could hoof the ball from one end of the field to the other. No wonder the golden boy of South African rugby was called 'Nasty Booter'.

The Lions can have no grumbles about their defeat. Although the scoreline was close, the try count was 5–1 in favour of the Springboks and the Lions depended greatly on fly-half Tony Ward, who notched 18 points from five penalties and a dropped goal.

Eventually, the Lions lost the series 3–1 but had the consolation of winning every provincial game – an achievement in itself. Whether I would have made the Test side or remained a regular midweek 'dirt tracker' can only be surmised. A betting man would not have given me good odds because Graham Price, the Welsh tight head, was an outstanding forward and had the experience of appearing in all four Tests in New Zealand three years earlier.

On the other hand, anything can happen on tour. Coach Mike Doyle often exhorted the 1984–85 Irish

75

Triple Crown side to 'give it a blast' and I would have adopted exactly that attitude in South Africa. I had nothing to lose. In fact, I understand my replacement, Ian Stephens, of Bridgend, was very close to selection for the fourth Test at Loftus Versveld – quite an achievement for a player better known in Wales as a loose head.

I still feel Noel Murphy's 'killer' approach early on was very wrong. But both he and Syd Millar were great personalities and there were times when we had plenty of fun. Murphy was also extremely sympathetic when a player had a serious problem and offered cheerful encouragement if anyone felt a bit despondent because of an injury.

Many people ask my view on apartheid. And my answer is unequivocal. I detest it. I've walked along the seafront in Durban and seen the 'Whites Only' and 'Blacks Only' signs and these left a deep impression.

So why did I agree to take part in a tour which was opposed by so many people? My view is that it is far too easy to pick on sportsmen and push them to the forefront of the argument. What about all the multi-national companies from all over the world who have bases in South Africa and make billions of pounds as a result? If governments decided to take apartheid seriously and refused to invest in South Africa, rugby players like myself would feel a moral duty not to go.

I don't agree with South African government policies. But neither do I support much of what happens in many South American countries and in the eastern bloc.

The Lions tour, as I have indicated, was my Olympic Games – the pinnacle of my career. Whether or not we had gone, I don't believe it made the slightest difference to what is happening in South Africa. The Americans pulled out of the Moscow Olympics – but the Russians are still in Poland and Afghanistan.

You will not beat apartheid by making political capital out of sportsmen. Take away the foreign-owned banks, mining companies, agricultural concerns, technical knowledge and all the rest and we might see an appreciable change.

All out warfare – the Australian and England packs slug it out during the Second Test, with Andy Ripley looking on in disbelief

Punch-up against Wales. Geoff Wheel and Bill Beaumont clash angrily while Allan Martin and I prepare to intervene

England's proud Grand Slam squad, pictured before their thrilling victory over Scotland at Murrayfield

Leading from the front – skipper Bill Beaumont on the rampage at Murrayfield, with Roger Uttley and Fran Cotton in support and Scotland's Mike Biggar trailing behind

With the Lions in South Africa (left). We were flogged to death during the first week's training camp here at Vanderbijlpark. Note the stockinged feet – most of us were too blistered to wear boots!

The end of my brief career as a Lion (right). Skipper Derek Quinnell assists me from the field at East London

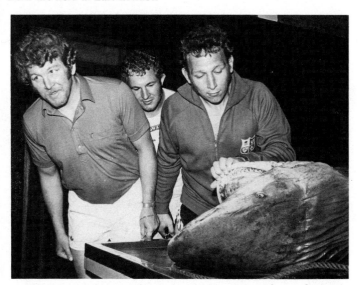

Graham Price (left), myself and Clive Williams come face to face with Jaws! The shark was due to feature on the menu at the Lions' hotel in Durban

A fearsome, if rare, sight of Blakeway, with the ball in hands, spearheading an England attack! It happened during our tremendous 1982 victory in Paris. John Scott (left) and Peter Wheeler are battling to keep up with me

The French get rather shirty with me during the same game in Paris

The first Test was over and I headed for home. I felt desperately disappointed and yet, as it happened, I would not have completed the tour even if I had steered clear of injury.

There were three weeks of the trip remaining when I suffered severe stomach pains and was rushed to hospital. The problem was a familiar one – torsion of the bowel – and so I underwent major surgery for the third time in my life. I can well remember waking up in my hospital bed, looking up at the television news and seeing the Lions arriving back in London. You could spot my replacement, Ikie Stephens, laughing and joking, just as he always does. There was Phil Orr too, the man who had filled the gap left by Fran's departure.

I was not long out of hospital before my thoughts turned towards playing rugby again – but it was likely to be a fair time before I made a full recovery. All I could do was walk and walk in the hope of regaining a modicum of fitness. 'What have you been up to?' asked the surgeon in ominous tones when I returned for a check-up. Oh no, I thought, he's going to tell me to call it a day.

Fortunately, the news was encouraging. 'Whatever you've been doing since the operation, keep it up,' he said. 'The wound has healed well on the outside but it will need time inside. I shouldn't plan to play any rugby for another year.'

Sensible advice was ignored. I was hungry for more action which was hardly surprising because, since breaking my neck in October 1977, I had played only a handful of matches.

The 1980–81 season was not very old when the Gloucester side once again took the field in front of the Kingsholm faithful with Blakeway in the front row. I must have been crazy! My stomach wall was obviously still very weak because the scar soon split in places and was weeping – and yet still I carried on. I was also aware of a back problem which gradually became severe.

That season, I was often to play in considerable pain. The medical experts tell me that the stomach wall has a role in supporting the back – and in my case it just couldn't take the pressure. There was, however, a job to be done. Neary and Uttley might have called it a day but the rest of the Grand Slam side was still together and convinced that England's dismal record of failure at the Arms Park would be halted in the first game against Wales. It might have done if this match had not marked the end of the road for Fran, helped off in the fifteenth minute with a torn hamstring and never to play again.

His loss, as I have already described, heralded a first cap for Bristol's Austin Sheppard. As he was considered very much a tight head in those days, I took my England bow as a loose head, facing my Vanderbijlpark adversary Graham Price once again in an eyeball-to-eyeball confrontation.

In my view the reorganized England front row coped well. And while I couldn't be expected to get much change out of a wily old bird like Pricey, Wales gained no great advantage from us. The game was a cracker and with Dusty Hare's siege-gun right boot serving us magnificently – he scored five penalties in addition to claiming our only try – we still had our noses in front near the end.

In a broader sense, however, England's confidence had been undermined. Pressure from Wales was taking its toll. As we prayed for the final whistle, Clive Woodward suffered a fatal lapse of concentration and wandered offside. The whole of Wales howled for a penalty which was awarded and kicked by Steve Fenwick.

Wales was ahead 21–19 and yet there was still time for us to force another penalty with the very last kick of the afternoon. Could Dusty do it again? Not this time. Perhaps it was poetic justice that the ball sailed wide because we had been so lucky that the Leicester full-back rescued us in identical circumstances against the old enemy a year before.

Poor Woodward. He felt sick. But I don't believe he should shoulder the blame. England was on the ropes at the time and any one of us could have offended.

For the first time in a major international, I had tasted defeat. It meant there was even more pressure to beat

Scotland in the next match at Twickenham and, despite the aching back, I was ready for an introduction to Gala prop Jim Aitken. The game was one of the most entertaining at Twickenham for many a long year, each side scoring three tries and Cambridge University student Huw Davies marking this debut with a most accomplished performance at fly-half. Colin Smart, who had been through the mill with Newport, had the unenviable task of succeeding Fran and Bristol's Bob Hesford made his first appearance as a replacement when another newcomer, flanker Nick Jeavons, was injured.

Confidence was restored with a 23–17 win, Davies grabbing the decisive late try after some delightful work by the ever-creative Mike Slemen.

England won in Ireland as well by 10–6 although this was another nightmare occasion for me. After twenty-two minutes, I suffered a neck injury which caused immediate concern because it left me with no feeling at all in one arm. In view of my history, I was taken off and rushed to hospital where nobody appeared too worried. Everyone seemed to be more interested in watching the match on the box and, after being told there was nothing to fret about, I hitched a lift back to Lansdowne Road.

I arrived to discover that England had won, even though Smart, nicknamed Grand Sumo because of his generous girth, was by no means at ease on the tight head. My injury had meant a long-awaited first cap for Gordon Sargent, prompting wild celebrations in Lydney and Gloucester. The big snag was that the Old Forest Bear and the Grand Sumo were both specialist loose heads – and they chopped and changed all afternoon trying to work out how best to cope with the Irish.

I was thrilled for Sarge, who had been on the bench throughout the Grand Slam season without getting a game. He really thought his big moment had come in Paris the year before when I was booted in the ribs; he would willingly have leapt straight from his seat four tiers up in the Parc des Princes stand if there had been a cap in it. Later on in Dublin, I congratulated him. 'Here's that quid I owe you,' he joked.

My back and neck problems were now a matter of great concern to the England selectors. The match against France at Twickenham followed two weeks later and, when the team was announced, there was no Blakeway . . . just A. N. Other. Budge Rogers had reached the stage at which he would no longer take my word that I was match fit. I had to return to Ray Davies at Gloucester Royal Hospital and obtain a letter confirming that I was capable of playing and at no more risk than any of the other twenty-nine players. The letter was handed over before a training session – and I stayed in the side.

The French succeeded in shutting one of my eyes early on. But that didn't bother me – the back still hurt and I just wasn't capable of soaking up pressure as I had done in the past. We were 16–0 down by half-time after playing into a howling gale and again I contemplated going off. This would hardly have gone down well, however, and so I stuck it out. England rallied but France held on to triumph 16–12 and succeed us as Grand Slam winners.

This match was to feature probably the worst refereeing blunder I have known. It not only cost England possible victory but also wrecked our chances of at least sharing the International Championship.

The French were leading 3–0 when they craftily took a quick line-out on the left and Berbizier and Rives put the Beziers forward Pierre Lacans over. There was no way it should have been allowed because hooker Pierre Dintrans grabbed a completely different ball from a ball-boy, which is not permitted in the laws. Even the original ball could not have been used so quickly because it had been handled by the crowd and was still high up in the stand.

We knew full well it wasn't a try. So did the touch judge. Unfortunately, Scottish referee Alan Hosie seemed to be the only person who hadn't cottoned on. Bill Beaumont went up to speak to him but was waved away. Hosie stood arm aloft to signal the try.

I could have killed him. Bill, to his credit, refused to make a fuss afterwards. 'That's just the rub of the green,' he told the journalists. But the other lads were fuming.

We were playing purely for the honour of representing England, not for financial reward. In an international season, you stand or fall on what happens in just four games. I accept that Hosie thought he was doing the right thing – and, whatever the circumstances, the referee's decision is final. But it was a dreadful clanger which even now makes me seethe.

Over a period of weeks leading up the French match, I had been receiving manipulative treatment for my back from the highly respected Hemel Hempstead sports physiotherapist Terry Moule. He has helped people like Roger Uttley, golfer Brian Barnes and athlete Sebastian Coe. He also worked on shot-putter Geoff Capes, although how on earth you go about manipulating that lot I'm not quite sure!

For all Terry's skill, the back was no better. My enjoyment of rugby had been blunted as a result. I couldn't survive any longer and, when the subject of England's forthcoming tour of Argentina was raised on the night of the French match, I told Budge Rogers I wouldn't be there.

In hindsight, it would have been sensible merely to say I wasn't available. But I was so depressed that I announced my retirement. The 'bump and grind' of rugby had become too much for me, I explained in subsequent press interviews.

Blakeway had quit – or so I thought – for the second and last time.

7

Back in the Fray

The retirement did not last long. As the summer came to an end, I yearned once more to pull on a Gloucester shirt and, hopefully, add to my collection of England caps.

By November, I was taking a familiar road – to Camborne. Gloucestershire, distinctly miffed to be hammered 21–7 by Somerset at Bath, dropped half the side and installed Gloucester team-mate Malcolm Preedy and myself in the front row against Cornwall. We should have steamrollered the Cornish for a second time, but Gloucestershire won only 10–6 and were extremely fortunate to scrape through the South-West group of the County Championship on points difference.

Later that month, Gloucestershire took on Lancashire at Bristol in the semi-final. Lancashire won again in another tight match, but at least there was an opportunity to chat with Beaumont, Smithy, John Carleton and Mike Slemen.

By December, I was playing for the Rest with Colin Smart in an England trial. We did enough to persuade the selectors to promote the Newport player for the Australian international, which England won 15–11. Gary Pearce had established himself as senior tight head in Argentina. My big moment came a few days earlier when, for the first time, I was asked to be captain in a major game – South and South-West Counties against the Wallabies at Kingsholm.

The game should never have been played. Cinderella on icé may be great entertainment for the kids at that time of year. But this was showpiece rugby in the foulest

82

of Arctic conditions. As Aussie skipper Mark Loane said in his speech after the match, 'We expect grass burns but never thought we would suffer ice burns as well.'

It was typical of the way English rugby approached such matches at the time that we were totally ill prepared. The Australians – including three Ella brothers – had been playing together for weeks. My team met for the first time on the morning of the match, a hopeless situation. I'm glad to say that, since then, the RFU's South-West technical administrator Chalkie White has done much to bring about substantial improvements in this respect.

What sort of a skipper I made, I'm not sure. But my approach was straightforward enough: 'I expect each player to give every ounce of effort he can produce.' They did. But we were still outgunned 16–3 – and I didn't even last the course.

Through taking my new responsibilities so seriously, I failed to concentrate sufficiently on basic essentials of front-row play like keeping an eye open for trouble. I was so keen to move on from one set piece to another that I turned my head away and was clobbered by a real haymaker, breaking my nose. I managed to keep going until half-time but had been swallowing a lot of blood and choking and so called it a day. Austin Sheppard trotted out once again as replacement.

England's championship season began with a 9–9 draw at Murrayfield, Andy Irvine's long-range, last-minute penalty rescuing the Scots. We were not to know that this would be Bill Beaumont's final appearance. Soon after, he retired on medical advice after receiving a blow on the head in the county final against North Midlands at Moseley.

So chirpy Steve Smith was in charge when I was recalled, instead of Pearce, to face Ireland at Twickenham. We were beaten – more comfortably than the 16–15 scoreline suggests – and this was to become the year of the Irish, with new skipper Ciaran Fitzgerald inspiring his country's first Triple Crown for thirty-three years.

I didn't begrudge Ireland its success. It had a typical tear-and-rush pack, featuring the old brigade of Fergus Slattery, Willie Duggan, Moss Keane and Phil Orr, and an outstanding fly-half in Ollie Campbell, who excelled at Twickenham.

The Irish, it strikes me, go about things the right way. They have a strong youth set-up, often filling Lansdowne Road for schools' finals, and a sensible provincial competition. Mick Doyle's carefree 'give it a blast' approach applied to the national side in 1982 – and, with characters like Keane in the ranks, there was never any danger that team spirit would flag.

What a bloke he is! I remember Moss flying in for Bill Beaumont's retirement game and arriving at the ground in his dinner suit. He had been to a function the previous evening and got so involved that there had been no time to change. 'I've had one hell of a night,' he confessed in the changing room. He wasn't interested in discussing line-out signals. 'You won't even get the paper from under my feet because I won't jump that high.'

Moss can certainly sink a Guinness or two. I made the mistake of walking into a bar with him one night. He banged his fist on the counter and a pint whizzed down to him – and was gone before the barman could pour another. 'Mr Keane,' I thought to myself, 'I shall be leaving you shortly.' I had no intention of trying to keep up with him.

Another tremendous Irish character is Willie Anderson, who just can't help cracking jokes from the moment a game is over. He had once been locked up in Argentina for pinching a national flag during a tour and found himself at the centre of an international incident.

When the Australians toured Britain in 1984, they recruited the former Argentinian player Henrique Rodrigues to bolster their front row. At the dinner after Australia's match in Dublin, Rodrigues brought the house down by producing an Argentinian flag and presenting it to Anderson. For once, the Irishman was lost for words.

The next game took me back to France where, for the second time, the home selectors had done England a great big favour. Their choice at loose head for an international debut was 6 ft 4 ins, nineteen stones Jean-Pierre Wolff, of AS Beziers, who, according to the newspaper reports, was going to eat me alive. What the French had forgotten is that I am a short, fat dwarf as props go and, sooner or later, the big, bad Wolff had to come down to my height in the scrums. When he did, he suffered. I had an easy ride that afternoon and like to think it was a significant factor in an exhilarating 27–15 win.

The England side was changing fast. After trying Jim Syddall against Ireland, lanky Steve Bainbridge was given his debut in the second row as partner to the faithful Colclough. Another newcomer was elegant fly-half Les Cusworth of Leicester.

The most crucial selection, however, was at full-back. Having discarded Marcus Rose and lost Nick Stringer with a hamstring injury, England plumped yet again for Dusty Hare. This was the *sixth* time he had been recalled in an England career of thirteen matches – and how he relished the opportunity! Dusty contributed 19 points from five penalties and two conversions – exactly his tally in Cardiff the previous year.

Victory signalled another hazy night of jollifications. Champagne costs something like £75 a bottle in Paris. I can't say we actually bought any – but there were plenty of celebrating Englishmen who did and we were only too pleased to join in. It was a great evening.

Of all the international grounds I have visited, Paris is my favourite. Cardiff and Ellis Park are attractive in their own way; and there is always a special atmosphere at Murrayfield and Lansdowne Road. But when you run into the great oval stadium at Parc des Princes, the noise is formidable – you feel a bit like the Christians being thrown to the lions. Every band plays its own tune, there are firecrackers and klaxons everywhere and invariably a few cockerels let loose as well.

The final match of the 1982 international season took us back to Twickenham and another meeting with Wales – this time, thankfully, without all the nastiness of the previous home game. It was a big day for my old Lions sparring partner, Graham Price, who was setting a Welsh cap record for a prop with his thirty-seventh appearance. My loose head opponent, however, was Ian Stephens.

Luckily, we caught the Welsh on an off day. We started with the wind at our backs and were 11-0 up in twenty-six minutes, the highlight being a solo try by John Carleton who temporarily found himself playing as an emergency scrum-half and took on the defence from forty metres out to score. Wales came back at us towards the interval but there is no doubt that the loss through a shoulder injury of scrum-half Terry Holmes – Bridgend's Gerald Williams took over – was a body blow to their hopes. When Dusty kicked his third penalty of the afternoon, we had won 17–7.

The remaining major event of that season was the John Player Cup final at Twickenham – Gloucester's third, but my first for the club. Our opponents, Moseley, were considered the underdogs but didn't play like it because the score was locked at 9–9 after eighty minutes and so extra time was required.

Gloucester had scored 154 tries that year and often startled the Kingsholm regulars with their uncharacteristically fluent approach. But neither side really got going on the big day, mainly I feel due to the strictness of referee Roger Quittenton who refused to let the play flow.

In the extra period, Moseley fly-half Mike Perry nudged his side ahead with a tremendous long-range dropped goal and there was precious little time remaining when we were offered one last penalty chance.

This was the crunch moment for full-back Paul Ford, son of Peter, who had already kicked three earlier on. Paul had been handed the unenviable job of following all-time Kingsholm favourite Peter Butler, the club's record points scorer, into the side and for some reason there were sections of the crowd who took a dislike to him. They just wouldn't get off his back during that season and the youngster – entirely blameless – felt very low.

Our scrum-half, Steve Baker, had also taken some stick at Kingsholm on occasions. And as we waited for Ford to line up his kick, 'Bakes' said with feeling, 'I hope for his sake he kicks it. He deserves a break.' For a player to make such a sympathetic comment in that extremely tense moment was quite something – and happily Ford did find the target to square the match. We shared the trophy with Moseley – a slightly unsatisfactory end to a rather disappointing match.

The Yanks love their baseball and grid-iron football. But rugby? That's very much towards the bottom of the popularity charts, as I discovered during the following month when England set off on an eight-match tour of Canada and the States. Quite why the RFU decided to make this a full-blown affair I shall never know. It would have been useful for England B and ideal for the under-23s – but not for a team which had just given a good account of itself in the International Championship.

I labelled it the dirty tour. We had been warned beforehand by RFU secretary Bob Weighill not to expect all the comforts of other major ventures. What that meant was that we had to pay for laundry ourselves and also eat out each day on the modest allowance we were given.

The laundry business didn't go down at all well. One of the essentials of any trip is that you should have clean clothes and training kit whenever necessary. We had been provided with reversible training shirts – plain on one side and hooped on the other – and that was a good idea. But there was no way I was going to pay to have it washed and ironed every day.

On occasions, I shoved it in the bath and trampled on it like a dhobi. For the rest of the time, I ponged. We all did. And it was only after a team protest that the management relented and paid a laundry bill out of their own pockets.

The rugby wasn't up to much either. In this respect, the tour was a joke. England won all eight games, scored 352 points and conceded only 34.

I was a spectator for the opening game in Toronto when England annihilated Eastern Canada 52–3. The next match was the international against Canada at the Swangard Stadium, Vancouver. I played and we won

43–6 and the score would have been much greater but for the fact there was a narrow pitch and it was difficult to spread the ball wide and evade some direct, grid-iron-style tackling.

One of the highlights of the trip for me was watching the Seattle Seahawks American Football squad in action – those boys really put some effort into their game. I also enjoyed a visit to the Queen Mary. But the Yanks, only really interested in the big-money sports, are never likely to compete with us on the rugby field. There was talk of our meeting fearsome forwards. In the event, they were hopelessly equipped when it came to the essential requirements of winning possession – and the American full-back in the final international match in Hartford was slower than me! England won 59–0. And the Americans were lucky to score nil!

Overall, it was a bit like taking a second-rate package holiday and I wasn't all that excited about American food. The hotels were all right although we found ourselves in a real dive in New York. When we stepped outside, we were told not to turn left. Then one day there was a drug bust, a real Starsky and Hutch affair with gun-waving cops smashing down doors and making one hell of racket. I was not sorry to return home.

I didn't hurry back at the start of the 1982–83 season. The Fijians were in England for a tour but I could not work up much enthusiasm for playing in the South and South-West game at Redruth until Derek Morgan rang up and said, 'We would like you to turn out – as captain.'

So I went – and could hardly believe I was still in England when we arrived in Cornwall. What we didn't know was that the locals were up in arms over the refusal of the selectors to include any player from that neck of the woods.

In the past, it had been normal practice to give all counties at least token representation in the side. But this South-West XV was picked purely on merit and the Cornish were so mad that local big-wigs were telling people not to go – and not to support us. Even car stickers advertising the match had been doctored so that the words 'South-West' were deleted from the full title of the home team.

The men they felt should have been in the side were Cornwall lock Roger Corin, who had played with distinction for the Counties against the All Blacks on a previous occasion, and Roger Spurrell, a former Launceston and Plymouth Albion flanker who by now was the highly successful skipper of Bath.

Gloucester second row John Orwin, a no-nonsense Yorkshireman, couldn't wait to meet the rugby reporter from the local newspaper who had suggested that 'Roger Corin eats forwards like Orwin for breakfast.'

Despite the constant booing of the crowd – the Fijians were cheered all the way and must have wondered what was going on – we cruised to a 36–6 win. The match offered me a first glimpse of Stuart Barnes, subsequently capped by England at fly-half but operating as a nippy and effective full-back on this occasion.

'Chester' Barnes, who scored 17 points, was still at Oxford University at the time and on the point of leaving the Newport club to join Bristol. 'We'll find you a job in Gloucester, don't you worry,' I told him. 'Come and join us.' But he never did and only recently caused quite a stir in West Country rugby by moving on again from Bristol to John Player Cup champions, Bath. Barnes, I am sure, will be a quality player for England in years to come.

The Fijians did not win one of their ten games, failing – like the Americans – to come to terms with the skill and strength of British forwards. I can quite see why Fiji has such a big reputation in sevens because it has big men who run and handle very impressively. But in the fifteen-a-side game, there is an awful lot to learn.

By now, I was getting quite a taste for captaincy. To my surprise, Gloucestershire, who had been led so successfully in the past – and later on as well – by Mike Rafter, appointed me skipper for the opening match in the first division of the revamped County Championship against Yorkshire at Headingley.

This was the strangest of games. We must have had 95

per cent of the ball and yet only just scraped a 9–6 win thanks to two penalties and a dropped goal by the Bristol fly-half David Sorrell. Yorkshire included former England player Alan Old but its real danger-men were two wingers we didn't know a great deal about at the time – Rory Underwood and Mike Harrison, both subsequently to wear the England shirt. These lads are real flyers and, when we gave Yorkshire the ball on a couple of occasions near the end, they almost caught us off guard and plundered the most unlikely of victories.

Representative demands were becoming formidable. After going to Redruth and Headingley on consecutive Saturdays, I was off to Twickenham to play for an England XV against the luckless Fijians. By now the tourists were thoroughly demoralized. They were mere cannon fodder for the strongest available England side and, if everything had gone right, we would have hit the ton in points. In the end the score was 60–19, with another speed merchant, Bath wing David Trick, grabbing three tries, and my Gloucester team-mate John Gadd – making a good impression on the flank – scoring twice.

From Twickenham, I moved to the Memorial Ground, Bristol, to lead Gloucestershire to a far more straightforward County Championship victory over a poor North Midlands side. But all was not well ... retirement number three was imminent.

It was mainly due to problems back at Kingsholm. Gloucester was going through a particularly rough patch at the time and, smack in the middle of this non-stop October programme, I was asked to turn out in a Wednesday-night game at Pontypool.

I declined. Because I had been away so much, I explained, there were business and family matters which had to come first. In any case, I had no intention of getting up at the crack of dawn for work after what was certain to be a very late night in Wales.

This didn't go down at all well, perhaps because it had been made pretty obvious to me in the past that some people felt I didn't play enough rugby for the first team.

Gloucester crashed by more than 50 points in Wales

and, to make matters worse, I wasn't available to play for the club the following Saturday due to a private engagement. The affair came to a head on the Monday night. I admit I was not at my best, having started the day at 3 a.m. sorting loads of fruit and veg., worked in the office, weight-trained with team-mate Mike Teague at Gloucester Leisure Centre during the early evening and then done a full club training session at Kingsholm.

In a nearby pub afterwards, I was cornered by a Gloucester committee man who had a right go at me. It was all my fault, he said, that the club were in the doldrums; if blokes like me had shown true loyalty, Gloucester would still be riding high. I was furious and stormed off. On the following Thursday, I returned and said that, if this was really what people thought of me, I was quitting. And I did.

My view was that rugby was supposed to be a game you played for fun – and at that time all my enjoyment had been destroyed. I didn't expect people to shine my boots for me. On the other hand, I was still representing the Gloucester club whenever I wore a Gloucestershire or England shirt. And when you are playing frequently at the highest level, something has to give. Ask John Pullin about that. Pullin had a wonderful career embracing forty-nine England and British Lions appearances, yet in his prime he often managed no more than a dozen games a season for Bristol. He realized you could not possibly expect to do everything, soak up the bump and grind, and survive.

I still believe I was right. I had done my bit for rugby; that same Gloucester committee man probably had no idea that, after the Fijian game at Camborne, I got up very early the next morning and drove more than 300 miles to London to keep a promise to appear in a charity game.

Gloucester, I decided, could get on without me. Subsequent events were to show that perhaps the cause of the Kingsholm decline lay very much deeper. Gordon Sargent quit and returned to Lydney and even John Fidler, the most loyal of Gloucester servants, played out the season with Cheltenham junior club Old Patesians. Gloucester finished 1982–83 with its worst record for years and the only consolation was that hooker Steve Mills and lock Steve Boyle made their England debuts in a 13–13 draw with Wales at Cardiff. Boyle did well enough to stay in the side against Scotland and Ireland and then walk straight into the Lions' party to tour New Zealand.

8

Shattered Dream

My international career – eleven England caps and a
fleeting appearance for the British Lions – would indeed
have ended there and then ... but for the lure of
Australian gold.

I missed rugby all right. It had been such a big part
of my life for so long. But very soon I was totally immersed
in the family business, making up for much of the time
lost to rugby. My wife and young children were seeing
far more of me and other interests developed as well. The
England lads would not have recognized me – I had
dieted from a fighting weight of sixteen-and-a-half stones
to a sylph-like thirteen stones.

Then one day the telephone rang. A very good friend,
not entirely unconnected with the international rugby
scene, said a proposition would be put to me if I turned
up at an hotel in Bristol the following week. It involved
a great deal of money, he said – so naturally I was there.

Australian entrepreneur David Lord was attempting to
launch his professional circus. It was to involve teams
representing all the major rugby-playing nations of the
world and there were grandiose plans for tournaments
both Down Under and in England, Wales and Scotland.

Lord himself was present. And the sort of money he
was talking about – £90,000 a head for two years' work
– was quite astonishing. Certainly, it was enough to
persuade all the twenty or so English players at the Bristol
meeting to sign a form expressing their interest in the
venture. As far as I was concerned, this was perfectly
legitimate – there was no question of being classed as a

93

professional until the first pay packet was safely in my bank account.

From the very beginning, however, I had reservations about the whole affair. Although Lord talked with total confidence about raising the necessary finance, the sums just didn't add up.

If groups of twenty or more players in seven or eight different international squads were to earn £90,000 each, the costs would be astronomical. If he could work that miracle, I was quite happy. But the potential English mercenaries were soon getting their heads together and insisting they wanted something up-front – a bond guaranteeing the money would be available.

We formed a committee – a sort of trade union – and there was a Jersey bank account established to handle our riches. I wasn't one of the shop stewards; just a little old swede basher from Gloucester, that's me.

Fleet Street picked up the story, which had the hierarchy at Twickenham in a rare old panic. The RFU wrote to all leading players in very high-handed fashion – they said nobody must even talk to Mr Lord and that anyone signing anything, let alone receiving money, would be banned from the game for life. It didn't worry me; in fact, I was tickled pink to see so many people rushing around making all manner of enquiries.

My prime concern was to get myself fit again a bit sharpish. This certainly couldn't be done overnight. It takes a long time to build up muscles, but they soon turn to flab if you lay off for a while. Reputation wouldn't be enough for me to survive in the hurly burly of a professional circus involving most of the world's greatest players. I would have to be as fit and strong as at any time in my life and make myself a saleable commodity. My earning power could well depend on an ability to stay the course.

The circus controversy raged on in the newspapers. The All Blacks were really sold on the idea and the Australians too. Andy Haden, the giant New Zealand lock, was rumoured to have vast sums of money in a sealed vault . . .

So it was for all the wrong reasons that retirement was forgotten once again and I returned for the start of the 1983–84 season. In the end, of course, Lord's enterprise came to nothing. All it had achieved in my case was a return to full fitness and rediscovery of an appetite to play rugby.

My first move was to join a group of senior players from the South and South-West in August training stints at Taunton. Chalkie White rang up out of the blue and asked if I would like to attend.

Past differences with Gloucester were put aside and, after a few games for the club, I was asked to captain the South and South-West against the All Blacks at Bristol. At the time, I felt it was essential to turn out because, with the circus still very much a live issue, the occasion was an important shop window prior to earning some big money. So I played, despite a hamstring which niggled every time I tried squats in the gym.

This was, without doubt, a time for Gloucester to forget all the traumas of the previous season. Apart from Bath flanker John Hall, our club provided the entire South and South-West pack – a proud moment indeed. The Gloucester forwards were no. 8 Mike Teague, flanker John Gadd, locks Steve Boyle and John Orwin, prop Malcolm Preedy, hooker Steve Mills and myself. In addition, Gloucester supplied wing Richard Mogg. It's fascinating to note that, of the South and South-West XV, the consistent and underrated Mogg was the only player not to win a full cap at some stage in his career. Even the two replacements we used – Alan Morley for Chris Martin and Austin Sheppard for Preedy – had worn the England shirt.

The game would have gone down as one of the great events of Gloucester Rugby Club history if we had won. And that's exactly what should have happened. We took 70 per cent of the ball and swarmed all over the Blacks in the first half.

But we were beaten before the kick-off – by an instruction from afar. New England coach Dick Greenwood was convinced the only way the All Blacks could be defeated in the international at Twickenham was through a 'kick it in the air and chase it' policy. Divisional sides were told that this was the way they had to play – irrespective of whether the selected team was equipped to do it.

The South and South-West XV palpably were not. The selectors had quite sensibly gone for a mixture of a rugged forward base from Gloucester and the attacking flair of Bath, who provided full-back Martin, winger David Trick, centre John Palmer and fly-half John Horton. The little trickster Barnes was there too, picked out of position in the centre.

We failed dismally. Exactly the same policy had been tried in a practice game against Newbridge a few days earlier – and it didn't work then. On the big day we even kicked with an inviting three-against-two situation on offer. It was a crazy mess-up and, despite some harsh words at the interval, we seemed incapable of changing the style in the second half. All we did was boot the ball down the throats of the tourists and watch Stu Wilson and Steve Pokere run it back at us.

The All Blacks won 18–6, with coach Bryce Rope expressing his amazement at our approach. How could any team with so much good possession lose by such a wide margin?

Five days later, England faced New Zealand at Twickenham and I was on the bench. My good friend Gary Pearce, of Northampton, won the tight-head berth and I had no complaints – the Midlands, inspired by Dusty Hare's kicking, had beaten the tourists 19–13 at Leicester and Pearce was a member of that side.

This was by no means a great All Blacks team. The New Zealanders were in the process of rebuilding, having left behind Whetton, Haden and some of the big boys who had mauled the Lions during the previous winter. So England had high hopes of victory for the first time since Russian Prince Obolensky played his heroic part in the 1936 triumph.

All the optimism was justified. Although I might not have agreed with the Greenwood dictum, it worked for him and new skipper Peter Wheeler. Thanks to a first international try by Maurice Colclough – how he enjoyed that moment – and the inevitable boot of Hare, England won 15–9.

Unfortunately, it didn't take long for all the excitement generated by the New Zealand victory to evaporate. England opened its championship season at Murrayfield and crashed 18–6 to a Scotland side destined to win its first Triple Crown for forty-six years.

Ireland was the next opponent at Twickenham and out went Bath flanker Paul Simpson – rather unlucky after a rip-roaring start against New Zealand – injured Peter Winterbottom, Pearce, Huw Davies and, of all people, Mike Slemen. I was back for my twelfth cap in place of Pearce with John Hall, Bryan Barley, David Cooke and Yorkshire firecracker Underwood filling the other gaps.

The game went well from my point of view against old adversary Phil Orr, although we were disrupted in the front row when Gosforth's Colin White was injured after an hour. I moved over to loose head to accommodate beefy replacement Stuart Redfern, from Leicester, and again we coped – in fact, I can't say I ever experienced any real problems against the Irish. England went on to win a fairly undistinguished match 12–9, Ireland taking another step towards the wooden spoon.

We moved on to France and the newspapers wondered if I could make it three wins out of three in Paris. No such luck. When the French are on song, nothing will stop them. We competed reasonably well in the first half but were then overwhelmed, suffering a 32–18 defeat. It wasn't much better at Twickenham a fortnight later against Wales which was led with fire and fury by Newport hooker Mike Watkins. Paul Rendall and Andy Dun, both of Wasps, were newcomers to the England pack but the match was ruled by Welsh line-out forwards Bob Norster and Richard Moriarty and skilful fly-half Malcolm Dacey. Winger Adrian Hadley scored the only try of the afternoon in the second half and Wales won 24–15.

On the domestic scene, Gloucester wasn't even involved in the John Player Cup – still counting the cost of the

97

previous season when we failed to qualify through the RFU South-West Merit Table. But at least there was success in the County Championship. Gloucestershire had been a little fortunate to defeat Middlesex 13–12 in the semi-final at Kingsholm in November, but a four-month wait for the final (have you ever heard of anything so daft?) clearly did us no harm at all. The opponents were neighbours Somerset, providing a memorable day out to Twickenham for 26,000 West Country folk.

The outcome of the game was never in doubt and we romped to a 36–18 win – but I was very close to ruining it all by being sent off.

My problem was a cheerful character called Chris Lilley, one of several Bath reserve-team players drafted into an injury-hit Somerset side. Early on, we set up a tremendous eight-man shunt near the opposition line and loose-head Lilley had little alternative but to collapse it. Referee Fred Howard's whistle signalled a penalty – but to Somerset and not Gloucestershire. Even though I was never likely to put the scrum down in that situation, Howard said I was to blame.

The same thing happened when Lilley collapsed a second time, crashing down so quickly and so hard that I suffered a painful injury to an elbow and shoulder. After it had happened yet again, Howard threatened to send me off – I was livid.

Now I acknowledge that all manner of skulduggery goes on in the front row and there are occasions when you deliberately set out to con the referee and the opposition. But it is simple logic that, having battled inside the 22 and then achieved forward momentum at the next scrum, you are fairly unlikely to waste all that effort by a deliberate collapse. The aim is either to get the ball away as quickly as possible or go for a pushover try.

My role is to destroy my opposite number. If he isn't strong enough to hold on, he must be penalized. Having said that, I was most perturbed when I attended a referees' conference and heard it suggested that, if a loose head repeatedly collapsed the front rows because he could not take the pressure, it was the opposition tight head's responsibility to keep the scrum up. What nonsense! Take that idea to its logical conclusion and you end up saying that a winger with the pace of Rory Underwood must not run round his marker in case he makes him look a fool.

I'm afraid Mr Howard, despite his international experience, doesn't come top of my list of favourite referees. He was in charge of a John Player Cup tie a few years back when Gloucester had a great deal of difficulty in disposing of competition minnows Southend. I've still got the video tape of that game – and, for the life of me, I fail to comprehend many of the decisions.

Obviously, players have to come to terms with the referee, whoever he may be. In general, you soon pick up his strengths and weaknesses and the way he interprets the law – but Mr Howard baffles me.

Fortunately, the difference of opinion during the county final had no effect on the result. We monopolized the second half with Stuart Barnes kicking goals from everywhere and Alan Morley, the world's record try scorer, crossing twice to help swell his tally for club and county in that season to exactly 50 – not bad for a thirty-four-year old.

The day was even better for another veteran of the side. Gloucestershire should really be renamed Fidlershire because second row John Fidler was making his ninth and last appearance in a final, breaking a championship record he had held jointly with two great stalwarts of Warwickshire rugby, Phil Judd and George Cole. Wearing a Gloucestershire shirt always seemed to bring the best out of 'Fids'.

9

End of the Line

John Fidler was known affectionately as Officer Dibble in the Gloucester and Cheltenham areas on account of the twenty years he served as a local bobby. England acknowledged his undoubted rugby skills but only, it seemed, when matches were to be played on the other side of the world. He had won his first two caps in Argentina in 1981 and now, in May 1984, joined me on the flight to South Africa for an England tour which was hardly to prove an outstanding success.

Officer Dibble would be the first to admit he wasn't in the peak of condition. His ankles were playing up; indeed they were so bad that within a few months he was forced to quit rugby altogether and retire from the police force. He had tweaked a hamstring as well and it was to take hours to bandage him up for a game.

Everything was against us. The South Africans were desperate to prove themselves the world's top rugby nation; the fixture list, including Tests on consecutive Saturdays, was taxing; there was the altitude problem I had experienced four years earlier; and our team lacked many of the players who had served their country so well in recent seasons.

Derek Morgan was tour manager and Dick Greenwood coach with RFU president Ron Jacobs to handle the inevitable political aspects of the trip. These were the twenty-six selected players:

Backs: W. Hare (Leicester), N. Stringer (Wasps), A. Swift (Swansea), D. Trick (Bath), M. Bailey (Wasps), P. Dodge (Leicester), J. Palmer (Bath), S. Burnhill

(Roundhay), H. Davies (Wasps), J. Horton (Bath), N. Youngs (Leicester), R. Hill (Bath).

Forwards: M. Preedy (Gloucester), P. Rendall (Wasps), P. Blakeway (Gloucester), G. Pearce (Northampton), S. Mills (Gloucester), S. Brain (Coventry), J. Scott (Cardiff) capt., D. Cusani (Orrell), J. Fidler (Gloucester), J. Hall (Bath), G. Rees (Nottingham), P. Winterbottom (Headingley), C. Butcher (Harlequins), M. Teague (Gloucester).

John Scott faced a huge task in succeeding Peter Wheeler as captain. He didn't need reminding that twelve years before England, led by John Pullin, had toured South Africa and won a glorious victory in the only Test. It was one West Countryman succeeding another as skipper – but somehow the challenge this time looked even tougher.

England had picked two no. 8s – Chris Butcher and Mike Teague. So Scotty, the most capped player in that position in English rugby history, had to revert to the second row – a role he had once filled as a raw seventeen-year-old in a regional trial.

Scott is a great-hearted forward and gave everything he had on tour. But you don't often find him playing as a lock for his club, Cardiff. And, as was to become apparent, he is definitely not of international quality in that position.

The big problem was that he just could not get his head into the scrum and hold it there. In training, his ears were pinched and his face scraped – he looked a bit of a mess. And we still hadn't sorted things out properly by the time the first Test came along at Port Elizabeth.

This was a notable day for Gloucester because we provided the entire England front row – the first time this had been achieved by one club. Sadly, unlike the famous Pontypool front row in Wales, Malcolm Preedy, Steve Mills and myself didn't last. We were one-match wonders and dropped en bloc.

This, as I see it, was the problem. All hookers 'shut the door' when they move across to strike, their hips hitting the hips of the loose-head prop. In other words, there should be no daylight. Quite where the second row sticks his head, I'm not sure. It's not really my concern. But you are very soon aware if the lock hasn't sorted himself out properly. And Scotty just couldn't get it right.

The South Africans were well equipped to exploit any lack of organization in this area. Loose-head Preedy, who had earned his first cap after a good performance in a draw with Western Province, was up against Hempies du Toit, who weighed seventeen-and-a-half stones and had a twenty-three-stones monster called Rudi Visagie shoving behind him.

Naturally, as skipper, Scotty told new boy Preedy what he wanted – and the orders were to keep edging out so that the second row's head could get in. In doing so, du Toit turned through the gap with ample assistance from Visagie. As a result, hooker Mills was desperately hanging on and moving all over the place – leaving me with the hopeless task of trying to tie the whole thing down.

England lost 33–15 and the Gloucester front row was made the scapegoats. But I've looked at the film of the game many times and this shows that, even with the bandaged-up Fidler pushing behind me, there were occasions when we were still going forward on my side. It was only in the last twenty minutes, incidentally, that our resistance crumbled and the floodgates opened.

For the only time in my career, I was actually dropped by England. What upset me was that no one bothered to ask my opinion about what had gone wrong. As a fairly senior member of the tour party, I felt that this would not have been unreasonable – but the management stayed silent and I held my peace.

The announcement of the team for the second Test in Johannesburg hardly improved my humour. It was delayed – deliberately, I imagine – until the very last training session before the match. That in itself was unwise because it meant the selected side never worked together. Scott merely halted the practice and quickly read out the selection – with a front row of Paul Rendall, Steve Brain and Gary Pearce.

If that's the way to tell internationals on a major tour

that they are dropped, I'll eat my hat. In fairness to Derek Morgan, he did apologize afterwards – but surely he could have given me a hint beforehand. Derek is an excellent tour manager, but on this occasion got it wrong.

Sadly, England lost the second Test even more heavily. The score was 35–9 but goodness knows how many points the Springboks would have amassed if they had not become embroiled in a fracas, principally involving the volatile Harlequin, Chris Butcher. They spent twenty minutes trying to sort things out and just stopped playing rugby.

I watched from the bench and expected to be called on at any stage because Rendall was carrying a calf injury and, ultimately, was to need surgery to repair an Achilles tendon. But Rendall stuck it out and my only consolation came at the final whistle when the Springbok skipper walked up and said, 'Thank goodness you weren't playing – on either side of the scrum.'

In all honesty, I do not believe my presence in the second Test would have prevented another England defeat. But I might have held them up for a while longer. I felt very sick at being dropped, although by no means ready for the scrap heap. 'You haven't finished with me yet,' I vowed on the way home.

A second South African tour had not altered my position on apartheid. I was more aware of the problems this time and horrified that racial prejudice could be practised with the backing of a country's constitution.

Again, however, England's rugby tour had not affected the situation in any way. I am a sportsman – and not even a professional. If golfers, tennis players, boxers and the rest could go there to make money without any interference, I saw no reason why I should not play rugby purely for enjoyment. Unlike former Irish international Dick Spring – now a prominent member of his country's government – I have no political ambitions.

My determination to prove a point with the England selectors remained as strong as ever during that summer. I trained relentlessly, concentrating on making myself a little quicker around the park rather than sticking to pure strength work, realizing the direction in which rugby was developing.

It was all to no avail. In the Gloucester club final trial late in August, I dived over the top of a heap of bodies to scoop up the ball and landed awkwardly on my ribs. It didn't hurt that much. But at first I just could not move. It was some time before I squatted on all fours and then struggled with difficulty to my feet.

Fourteen crucial weeks were to elapse before I was fully fit again. I tried acupuncture, water treatment, tablets – the lot. But apparently I had ripped a cartilage, which can be much more serious than breaking a rib, and the only real cure was rest.

By the time I returned, Gloucester was on a real high. Former county fly-half Bob Redwood had finished as Gloucestershire coach to take charge at Kingsholm and, with John Fidler running the fitness side of things, the bad times of a couple of years before had been forgotten.

There was not much chance of a first-team spot – especially when the lads put 58 points on Coventry at Kingsholm. I was assisting the United against Coventry Extra Firsts at Coundon Road on that day and just couldn't believe the score. Gloucester selectors have never bothered too much about reputations. If the club had a winning combination, they stuck to it – and rightly so.

The Wallabies were on tour. The South and South-West Counties played the Australians at Exeter and I went along as a spectator.

Before that, coach Jack Rowell and Chalkie White asked me down to Bristol to run a counties' scrummaging session. At one point, we took a breather and I called the lads over. 'This,' I said earnestly, 'is your big chance to stake a claim for England places. The Exeter match will be the real showpiece before they pick for the international.'

Prophetic words, indeed. The South-West pack played so well – the Australians were a little fortunate to escape with a 12–12 draw – that no fewer than seven of them went on to win England places that season. Prop Gareth

Chilcott and second row Nigel Redman, both members of Bath's John Player Cup winning side, made their debuts against the Wallabies alongside Steve Mills and John Hall while Austin Sheppard, John Orwin and Bob Hesford featured later on. Only flanker Roger Spurrell – a very unlucky man – missed out.

Chilcott's career as England's loose head was to be short lived. The Bath lumberjack – strong, solid and brave – had been doing his best to live down a reputation as something of a rogue, having been sent off three times in his career and suffered one ban of a year. On all the occasions I played against Chilcott, I can't say I experienced any problems. But England, said the experts, would never pick him – unless, as was the case now, they had run out of genuine loose-head contenders.

Sadly, Chilcott's temper got the better of him at Twickenham. Towards the end he took a swipe at Australian scrum-half Nick Farr-Jones right in front of the referee and might even have suffered his fourth dismissal. The England hierarchy clearly did not like it because he did not feature again that season and, even when subsequently the selectors were scraping the barrel for loose heads to go to New Zealand, he was still ignored. One stupid and unnecessary act had cost him dear.

In many ways, I feel sorry for Chilcott. Off the field, he's a great guy and I recall enjoying a few jars with him after an England training session at Bisham Abbey. He has been an outstanding servant to Bath and didn't let England down against a magnificent Wallabies side who went on to perform their own version of the Grand Slam. On the other hand, can you afford to carry a man who is liable to land his side in trouble at any time?

His petulance against Australia could have made the difference between winning and losing a tight match. Even when the South-West Counties faced the Rumanians at Gloucester a few weeks later, Chilcott was up to his tricks. The ball was far away and the whistle had gone inside the tourists' 22 when he clattered into one of their players quite unnecessarily and sent him crashing into touch. I don't think he was even penalized – but what if

it had been an international and the touch judge had
intervened? Instead of being in a possible try scoring
move, England would have been kicked back to halfway
and perhaps even lost as a result. Selectors note this sort
of thing when they are studying individual players – and
so the Kingsholm match may also have contributed to
his rejection.

Chilcott's fall from grace was a stroke of luck for me –
although I hadn't a clue that I was about to be catapulted
back into the England side.

Once again, I watched the South-West Counties' New
Year match against the Rumanians from the replacements' bench, hardly giving a thought to the fact that
Derek Morgan and his committee would be naming a
side for the Twickenham international later that evening.
Apart from bringing in Steve Brain for hooker Steve Mills,
who damaged a nerve in his neck against Australia, I
anticipated no major changes.

Imagine my surprise, therefore, when people started
coming up during the after-match dinner, shaking my
hand and slapping me on the back. Perhaps they knew I
had just celebrated my thirty-fourth birthday? Then
skipper Roger Spurrell came in and said he had heard
that I was picked – at loose-head prop!

'You're kidding,' I said, thinking about Chilcott,
Huntsman, Rendall, Preedy and all the other men who
were in with a shout. But Spurrell's mole was right and
later that evening the news was confirmed.

I was thrilled. But I don't mind admitting it worried
me a bit as well. My career had started at Cheltenham
at loose head and I had played in the position on tour for
England in Australia and for Gloucester and the county. I
had also done the job as an emergency measure in full
internationals against Wales and Ireland. But did
England realize I had played just three matches in Gloucester colours that season? All had been at tight head –
twice for the United and once in the traditional Christmas
dust-up with Lydney. I even had a chest infection when
I faced Lydney, getting out of bed to play the game and
returning there immediately afterwards.

My only game at loose head before making a first full international appearance in the position was for Ross Second XV against Raglan in front of half a dozen spectators at Ross. We won 6–3 and I managed one startling burst down the middle, selling dummies galore! But this was hardly ideal preparation for meeting a side, who, not long before, had humbled Wales and Scotland in Bucharest.

Still, I had made it . . . from Ross Seconds to England in one jump! Never let it be said there isn't some useful talent around in junior rugby!

The England side had changed rapidly since South Africa. Paul Dodge was in charge and the selectors had taken the bold decision to blood new backs in Wasps wing Simon Smith, Liverpool and Cambridge University centre Kevin Simms, Cambridge fly-half Rob Andrew and Bristol scrum-half Richard Harding. The major shock, however, was the debut of 6ft 8ins, seventeen stones line-out forward Wade Dooley, a twenty-seven-year-old policeman who played for Preston Grasshoppers, Dick Greenwood's club.

Preston Grasshoppers? Sounded more like an American grid-iron outfit then a rugby club. Lads like John Orwin – still to win his international colours – were not in the least bit amused. When had the Grasshoppers last played at Pontypool or Aberavon on a wet and windy Wednesday night?

The press thought initially that his name was *Wayne* Dooley, showing how much they were aware of the newcomer. But, for once, I take off my hat to the selectors. Dooley might have been raw in many respects but he was to do a fair job for England in the 1985 season – and no doubt will mature into a top-class international forward in the future, provided England keep faith with him.

It was a sobering thought that I was now the oldest member of the England team, although Dodge and Gary Pearce had won more caps. I felt positively ancient as I changed next to Simms, a chirpy Lancashire lad who did not look his nineteen years. He had not even been born when I started playing rugby!

I laughed to myself when the centre was presented with his cap later on. If they had given him a satchel as well he would have looked like the original fifth-form schoolboy.

On the field, however, Simms was fearless in the tackle and extremely quick off the mark. Andrew impressed me as well although I felt it was appropriate for the veteran of the side to offer some sage advice when he was called up to take a penalty and subjected to some very unfair booing.

'Son,' I said, 'they have been booing me for years. I have had bread rolls and tin cans thrown at me, I've been spiked by a spectator's umbrella and been spat at as well. Don't worry about it.'

Andrew's response was perfect because he kicked the points. Afterwards, he said he felt we had been involved in an away match. 'There are a lot more hostile places than Twickenham,' I told him. 'You'll be well aware all right when you are away from home. I remember appearing for England against the Americans in New York when the organizers did not dare play the National Anthem in case it incited trouble from the local Irish community.'

Although the Twickenham crowd were not entirely satisfied, I felt that the new-look England side had performed pretty well on this first outing together. The tourists were difficult to play against, tackling with the commitment of a team determined to justify their first official international fixture against England and refusing to offer very much in the way of adventure themselves.

The scrummaging had been no problem. But it was to be a while before I was put to a more severe test in my new role. Snow in Dublin caused a postponement of the game with Ireland and so the next opponents were France at Twickenham.

Over the years, England have had a record of boosting players to the sky at one moment and knocking them down just as quickly. Thankfully, Derek Morgan and Richard Greenwood believe that patience and consistent selection are vital in building an outstanding side. And

Ireland's Moss Keane – a great character and highly respected opponent

Gloucester's John Fidler, complete with the inevitable heavy bandaging, playing for England against Western Province

Gloucester made rugby history when the club provided the entire England front row – Malcolm Preedy (right), hooker Steve Mills and myself – against South Africa in Port Elizabeth in 1984. Sadly, we were all dropped for the next Test

England's match against Rumania in 1985 marked my first full appearance as an international loose-head and brought a richly deserved debut for Gloucester skipper John Orwin (left)

Irish No. 8 Brian Spillane feeds scrum half Michael Bradley at Lansdowne Road. Ireland's victory clinched the international championship

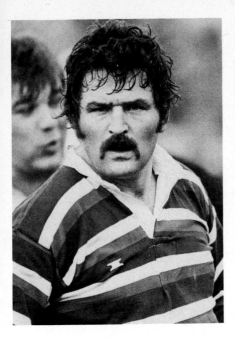

Robin Cowling, one of the experienced props at Kingsholm when I joined Gloucester. He moved on to Leicester and was capped by England

Captaining South and South-West Counties against the All Blacks at Bristol in 1983

The hurly-burly of a John Player Cup semi final against Coventry in 1982. Mike Teague, England's No.8 in New Zealand three years later, is the man with the ball

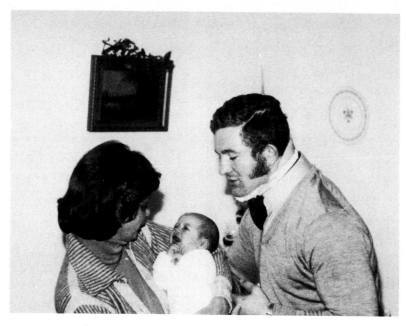

Happy and also painful memories of Christmas, 1977. My wife Ros and new
daughter Laura – and me in a neck brace

At home near Tewkesbury – Ros, son James and Laura

so the only change from the line-up which started against Rumania was the introduction of lanky Bath full-back Chris Martin for the injured Nick Stringer. Martin was yet another graduate of that South West XV at Exeter.

The French only had to turn up to win – or so the papers said. But we got amongst them a bit, making sure they could not settle, and, with Andrew kicking two penalties and a dropped goal, we drew 9–9.

This game will be remembered as Richard Harding's match. The sturdy Bristol scrum-half, known as 'Corky', had been around for a few years and thoroughly deserved his belated recognition. Undoubtedly he saved us from defeat by the French with his remarkable last-ditch tackle on Patrick Esteve, knocking the ball from the astonished winger's hands deep into the in-goal area. Harding went on to play in the next match against Scotland before being dropped. I wonder how long it is since an English scrum-half appeared in an unbeaten side for three games only to get the chop? Corky can count himself extremely unfortunate.

The other extraordinary feature of the French game – and the entire championship – was their amazing insistence on sticking to the outdated idea of using scrum-half Jerome Gallion to throw in while hooker Philippe Dintrans operated as an auxiliary scrum-half. It was never likely to give fly-half Lescarboura the ball at any great speed and reduced their options too. This was suicide by the French and in my view cost them the title.

Again, we scrummaged satisfactorily. But there were dark clouds on the horizon because I had needed pain-killers before the game to ease what was assumed to be a pinched nerve in my back. The discomfort spread to my neck by the time the Arctic winter relented and allowed the Scotland match to go ahead at Twickenham in March.

The injury had originated in January and I haven't a clue when it happened. Don Gatherer, shrewd as ever, thought my backache might be referred pain from the neck. What worried me increasingly was a gradual wasting of the muscles in my right arm, shoulder and pectoral area. One evening I went weight-training as usual with England replacement forward Mike Teague at Gloucester Leisure Centre. I picked up a dumbbell to perform an exercise I had done thousands of times – and my right arm just wouldn't go up.

Mike commented on how different I looked and for the first time I recognized there was something seriously wrong. Secretly, I went away for a month and pumped the weights hard five nights a week in a bid to rebuild my strength. But there was no improvement. In fact, it deteriorated even more.

We won the Calcutta Cup game 10–7, although hardly in scintillating style. Simon Smith scored a try – England's first at Twickenham for ages – and Andrew kicked two more penalties to edge us home. But, as happened throughout the season, we won decent possession in fits and starts and failed to make full use of our dangerous backs.

Scotland also squandered victory in a pantomime sequence at the end when the ball was hacked through and anyone of half-a-dozen players had a chance to pick up and score. Rory Underwood somehow managed to intervene as I watched disbelievingly somewhere back on halfway.

The results against France and Scotland emphasized just what a fine line exists between triumph and failure in international rugby. Englishmen still bask in the glory of the Grand Slam year – and conveniently forget how Dusty Hare robbed the Welsh at Twickenham. Ciaran Fitzgerald was awarded the Lions' captaincy in New Zealand in 1983 on the strength of Ireland sharing the International Championship with France. But the Lions' whitewash led to him being ditched by his country the following season – and Ireland claimed the wooden spoon.

Fitzgerald had the last laugh, of course, in 1985. The winter weather enabled the Irish, fresh from a glorious 21–9 victory over Wales at Cardiff, to wrap up the Championship by defeating England at Lansdowne Road.

By now, my neck and back were really sore after any game. I was still on the medicine and Dick Greenwood

110

had noticed the change in the shape of shoulder and arm. 'You are like a tennis player, with one side bigger than the other,' he said.

I made light of it, of course, and prepared to win my nineteenth cap. Despite my problems, I had no thought that this would be my farewell to rugby. It was nice to think that Phil Orr, present in the Irish front row on my debut day five years earlier, was still there. For the first time in the season, I was on an international pitch with someone older than myself.

But Orr, the great warrior from Old Wesley, was to outlast me. The Irish never threatened us in the tight; the game was settled primarily in the line-out and loose. But they had all the luck that was going on the day – the narrow divide between victory and defeat – and Michael Kiernan's late dropped goal settled it. It was 13–10 to Ireland and the whole of Dublin celebrated.

England still had to face Wales at Cardiff, a match postponed from February. Briefly, I looked ahead and thought of avenging the narrow defeat suffered in Fran's last game. But I was not going to make it.

Gloucester was due to visit Neath. As I had only just reclaimed a regular first-team place, displacing Malcolm Preedy for an epic John Player Cup semi-final against Bath at Kingsholm, I was keen to play.

Once more, I telephoned for an appointment with Ray Davies at Gloucester Royal Hospital and went through the inevitable X-rays. His assistant showed me the results and looked glum. The vertebrae on the neck were supposed to be clear – and were not. And one, as she put it, was 'in a bit of a mess'.

'What has been going on then?' asked Mr Davies a few minutes later. I explained how I had been relying on medication to play. I still felt I could keep out of trouble sufficiently to survive in club rugby – but knew there was no hiding place in an international. The questioning continued: 'Can you play without the pills?' I admitted I could not and he said quietly, 'Well, I wouldn't then.' And that was it.

Twice before in my life, I had visited Mr Davies fearing

that my rugby career was in ruins. On both occasions he had offered me hope – even when my broken neck was still in a plastic collar.

Now, he was talking differently. Apparently, I had pinched two nerves and it was recommended I go into traction for a month and then see him again.

I went home and talked it over with Ros. I would have to call it a day, we agreed, and so I contacted Gloucester chairman of selectors Alan Brinn and cried off the trip to Neath.

The England squad was meeting in London that weekend. I rang Derek Morgan at the Petersham Hotel and told him I was quitting. 'Oh dear, oh dear,' he kept saying, obviously wondering as we talked who would take my place against Wales.

For a while, I made myself scarce as far as inquisitive Fleet Street journalists were concerned and Ros made all sorts of excuses on my behalf. England didn't want the truth to come out just yet. Eventually, I pleaded with Derek Morgan for Twickenham to come clean and tell the full story. Not long after, the official announcement was made – and Blakeway retired for the fourth and last time.

10

Troublemaker

The crime files of Gloucestershire Rugby Union show that I was sent off twice during the early stages of my career. But I can now reveal that it happened three times – although, much to my relief, this additional occasion was very much hushed up by the Gloucester club.

It occurred in a Gloucester trial not long after I joined and no player before or since has suffered such an indignity. These games tend in any case to be rather rugged affairs because this is the big opportunity for players to establish seniority – perhaps for months to come.

I had taken particular exception to the aggressive attitude of another senior forward, who was threatening inexperienced newcomers and, at one point, laid one of them out. The action was totally uncalled for and so, as the ball was kicked away, I hit him hard on the jaw.

Unfortunately, Nick Jones, the referee from the Gloucester Society, saw what happened and had little alternative but to order me off.

I don't mind admitting I was a bad lad in the early days. To an extent, any young prop must expect quite literally to fight for survival on occasions; there is always the old-timer who is only too anxious to sort out any upstart who might threaten his place.

But a youngster must, at the same time, exercise a certain amount of restraint and acknowledge there is a tough apprenticeship to be served. This, I have to say, wasn't always my way of going about things. In fact, thinking back, I was a right tearaway.

The first sending-off happened as a greenhorn with

Cheltenham – and was responsible for my quitting the club. We were playing Lydney, never the mildest of opposition, and one of their forwards kept poking his fingers in my eyes. My inexperience was quite apparent because after a while I told the referee, 'If he does that again, I'll thump him. You stop him, or I will.'

It's not the sort of thing you should say to any official. Inevitably, the gouger struck again. I whacked him and the Cheltenham lads moved away. Unfortunately, my assailant remained on the floor. I was called over and awarded the early bath.

At the time, there was no automatic thirty-day ban. Mike Burton, another player with a lengthy county disciplinary file, had just received a paltry five-day suspension so that he could resume hostilities the following Saturday. Gloucestershire also backdated a ban on Cheltenham hooker David Protherough – later the Gloucestershire coach and a player and coach of Moseley – and so he kept on playing.

In the case of the unknown Blakeway, however, the treatment was very different. I was given six weeks! I couldn't believe it. Shortly afterwards, my fury increased when it transpired that the Cheltenham secretary had been away on holiday and the letter notifying the club of the hearing had not even been opened. So no one was there to put my case from start to finish and I was left totally in the dark.

That was it, I decided. I dashed off a letter to Cheltenham, saying that if this was the way they looked after the interests of their players, I was going. And so off I went to Kingsholm.

This, it transpired, was the beginning of the rather sad decline and fall of Cheltenham, formed in 1889 and proud of a history which included a visit by the 1905–6 All Blacks to the famous Athletic Ground. The club had an exceptionally strong fixture list until the early 1970s, but my departure sparked off an exodus of men like county centres Bob White and Paul Tait, John Fidler and Bob Redwood.

As a result, Cheltenham had several dreadful seasons

and, despite a move since then from the Athletic Ground to the brand new Prince of Wales Stadium, they struggle even now to recapture former glories.

My next brush with the county disciplinary committee followed within a year or so of transferring to Kingsholm when, ironically, I was sent off against Cheltenham. I was trying to get even with a Cheltenham second-row forward for an incident early in the match. But somehow it developed into a no-holds-barred fracas involving my rival prop John Hamer, a red-haired fireball who was later to play with distinction for Coventry. Trouble is that I have always been quick with my hands and slow with the brain. The referee halted the brawl and we both went off. I served five weeks that time.

The impetuosity of the hungry young man had got the better of me again. Although I probably didn't realize it at the time, the third sending-off had a salutory effect. It was obvious my aggressive instincts had to be curbed – certainly when it came to slugging it out in front of the referee – and gradually I calmed down.

As you get older, it becomes clear that it doesn't pay to be permanently involved in aggro. There are occasions, of course, when someone sets out to have a crack at you. Often, it's a youngster who, just like the wilder Blakeway of the early years, fancies making a name for himself against an established player.

Sometimes you let him get away with it, sometimes not. Inevitably, there comes a point where you can't just sit back. Generally speaking, however, the front-row union tend to look after one another in club rugby. Certainly, there may be the odd flare-up early on. But the guys you play year in and year out don't normally bother that much and get on with the game.

International matches are different. There's everything to play for and it's surprising how much undercover violence goes on. When I sat watching the clash between Wales and England after finally hanging up my boots, this was alarmingly obvious. Welsh second-row Robert Norster, for instance, could easily have been ordered off. He was struggling in the line-out early on against Wade

Dooley and it was clear to me that, very soon, the England lock would be picked on – and he was.

It's still possible to land in deep trouble, however, even when you are totally innocent – as I found to my cost once in a Gloucester game at Nottingham.

Early on, there was quite a bit of ill feeling between the sides and, after second-row Steve Boyle had been warned, our prop Alan Brooks was sent off for kicking. Later on, a Nottingham forward injured a knee and was off briefly for treatment. And I thought nothing more of this until someone showed me a national newspaper the following Monday.

'England thug stamps on Nottingham player,' was the theme of the article, going on to quote a home-club official to the effect that I had deliberately trodden on this player's knee and could have severed a ligament. There was talk of legal action against me.

I recalled the injury all right and the ruck in one corner when it happened. Yes, we had driven over the player. But are you supposed to stop in a situation like that and ask, 'Excuse me, would you mind moving your knee while we run over the top of you?'

The report was an absolute lie and written by a journalist who was neither at the game nor man enough to ring up and ask my opinion on the matter. He had merely reported comments from a Nottingham official who should have known better, ignoring that the injured player pushed in the scrum and jumped in the line-out without any apparent discomfort after treatment. We had also shaken hands quite amicably afterwards.

Gloucester secretary Terry Tandy studied the report. I had been picked on because of my international reputation and would be well advised just to ignore it, he said. My only consolation was that the player involved apologized to me for the unwarranted publicity during the following season when Nottingham played at Kingsholm.

People often ask me which was the best front row I ever faced. And I have no doubt in nominating the French trio who played such a crucial role in their Grand Slam season of 1981.

Admittedly, this judgement is coloured by the fact that I was in agony with my injured back in the international that year and literally battled minute by minute to survive an ordeal. Even in the peak of fitness, however, Paparemborde, Dintrans – colourfully and accurately described as the Raging Bull by Peter Wheeler – and my immediate rival Pierre Dospital would have been a real handful. Dospital, from Bayonnais, who arrived on the international scene with something of a reputation as a rogue, had mellowed a fraction by 1981. But he was still one of the most awkward scrummagers I encountered.

In my brief spell as an international loose head, Iain Milne, of Scotland, posed a few problems in the 1985 game at Twickenham. I had not met a player of his calibre in that position – but I still reckon I out-thought him on the day. I very soon realized it would be hopeless to allow his bulk to rest on top of me throughout the game. And so I took a leaf out of the Australians' coaching manual and refused to go down until the very last moment. The aim was to get the ball away in an instant. As a result, Scotland was denied the opportunity of putting me on the deck and winning a penalty; all they could do was flash for the ball.

I'm sure any international prop will always say, however, that the toughest games were in the early days of his career. That certainly applies in my case.

As Cheltenham's young loose-head prop – I was never a tight head before moving to Kingsholm – I remember spending eighty minutes grappling with Mike Burton in a heavy defeat by Gloucester. The game didn't go at all badly from my point of view. But that wasn't the case on the day Cheltenham visited Bridgend.

John Lloyd, who won twenty-four caps for Wales between 1966 and 1973, was my tormentor that afternoon. At one scrum, he turned me inside out and then picked me up and asked, 'Are you all right son?'

On a later trip to Wales with Gloucester United, hooker Fred Reed and I spent the whole match against Cardiff Athletic bent double, watching the bugs crawl across the grass. I was playing loose head against another high-quality prop, Roger Beard, more recently the Cardiff coach. 'That was a right hammering,' I said to Fred afterwards. 'Yes,' he replied, 'but we didn't lose a head.' To Fred, that was all that mattered.

You never forget experiences like that. After each one, you go away and vow to take it out on someone else in years to come. I've done so many times.

11

Glorious Gloucester

Digger Morris bears the scars of hundreds of battles fought in the name of Gloucester Rugby Club. I bet his wallpaper at home is cherry and white, the Gloucester colours.

The modern rugby player, he will tell you, is a pampered softie compared with the tough nuts who played with him in the pack before the last war. But this Kingsholm veteran has a heart of gold. His local team is Coney Hill, although no Gloucester home match takes place without Digger mounting a familiar and formidable guard at the entrance and later offering an analysis of where everything went wrong.

For me, Digger sums up the Gloucester rugby man. He eats and drinks the sport. Digger's son was a player for the club and over the years the old man has seen dozens more Coney Hill men graduate to Gloucester colours and then, sooner or later, return to offer their experience and further service to the junior side.

I am proud to have served Gloucester, although I could never hope to emulate Digger. An outsider would struggle to appreciate the impact Gloucester Rugby Club has on the city. Quite apart from the fact that Kingsholm is a toe punt away from the main shopping area, the city has never boasted a soccer team of anything more than modest non-league standard.

To watch league soccer – as if anyone from Gloucester would want to do so – you have to venture to Bristol or the Midlands. So rugby dominates the place. In my view, the atmosphere on a big match day compares with any major soccer venue. Part of the joy is that the team is very largely home produced. So when you pull on a Gloucester shirt, you are in a sense representing the interests of the many local clubs whose great delight is to see one of their number in the big time.

The development of John Player Cup rugby over the last decade or so has emphasized the point. The likes of Gordon League and Matson were unheard of much beyond Gloucestershire until they qualified for the competition through the county cup and immediately began ruffling the feathers of a few first-class sides. In 1985, Berry Hill took a turn and gave a very good account of itself in the third round against the eventual champions Bath.

Cup rugby was really tailor-made for Gloucester when it was introduced in the early 1970s. A hard, competitive edge was already long established at Kingsholm, as proved when the club beat Moseley 17–6 in the first Twickenham final.

Bristol had been ripped apart 15–4 at the Memorial Ground in the second round and then the Fleet Street rugby writers sat up and took notice when skipper Mike Nicholls – an extremely competent hooker and driving, inspirational skipper – took his team to Old Deer Park to demolish a London Welsh side with half-a-dozen British Lions. I didn't see the game but the thousands of Gloucester folk who flocked there insist it was one of the greatest performances in the club's 112-year history.

Since then, I've had the privilege of playing with all that side. A fearsome pack included Mike Burton, Robin Cowling – later to win international honours with Leicester – current chairman of selectors Alan Brinn and that wonderful flanker John Watkins, who had the distinction of playing in victorious England sides in South Africa and New Zealand in 1972 and 1973.

Mickey Booth, a comedian on and off the field, but the most astute of players, pulled the strings at scrum-half, with John Bayliss smashing down anyone who tried to go through the middle and Bob Clewes running in tries consistently on the wing.

Burton has had a controversial and tempestuous career. Long after the Battle of Brisbane, he made headlines again with his autobiography and revelations about the Adidas boot scandal which set the taxman in hot pursuit of star players and caused a fair old rumpus in quite a few international dressing rooms.

I still retain enormous respect for Burton, however, who technically was as good a tight-head prop as I have encountered. He taught me a great deal – and there was no man who cared more about Gloucester rugby.

In the early years of the national knock-out, Gloucester drew a tough tie away to Gosforth, whose side included players like England flanker Peter Dixon, Scotland hooker Duncan Madsen, David Robinson, who is now coach of the North side, and Malcolm Young, later the England scrum-half on ten occasions.

I was replacement but very soon called on to operate at loose head after Gordon Sargent suffered a groin injury. We lost a very controversial game 3–0, with our players and supporters convinced that referee Norman Sanson – fresh from sending off Willie Duggan and Geoff Wheel in an international – had disallowed a couple of perfectly good Gloucester tries.

The atmosphere was ugly at the final whistle. And the fact that players and referee had to walk several hundred yards to the distant Gosforth changing rooms hardly helped matters, because the crowd included a small group of drunken idiots who were clearly gunning for Sanson.

Burton, as much aggrieved by the result as anyone, spotted the danger. He called me and shouted, 'Stand here.' Then, as Sanson approached the double doors, Burton and I escorted him to the safety of the bar, pushing away the troublemakers at the same time.

Now Mickey Burton has a lot of faults. But he stood firm in the defence of Gloucester RFC on that day. Who the troublemakers were, I don't know. There is not much doubt that Gloucester would have been blamed, however, had Sanson been attacked. We could have been banned from the competition for ever more.

Occasionally these days, young Gloucester players have

a moan to me about a selection decision. That's inevitable at any club. But they don't get much sympathy. Some of Gloucester's finest players of the past decade or so form the committee – and I have the greatest respect for every one of them.

In addition to Brinn, Mike Nicholls is still there along with Jim Jarrett, a second row in the 1972 cup-winning side who also captained Pontypool. Ex-threequarters Richard Jardine and Bob Clewes provide expert knowledge on back play. And of course there's Bob Redwood, who had the distinction of helping Gloucestershire win the County Championship in the roles of player and coach. All made at least 200 first-team appearances and offer a wealth of experience and an ideal balance. They are certainly more than a match for any complaining youngster.

Jim Jarrett cropped up at the start of my career – and landed me in hot water. My debut was at Ebbw Vale against a Welsh side who included centre Arthur Lewis, just back from the 1971 British Lions tour of New Zealand, and hard-bitten forwards like Denzil Williams and Gareth Howells.

The Ebbw Vale pack were giving us a bit of a hard time. And after a while Jim muttered, 'Whatever I do in the next line-out, you do the same.' When the big moment came, Jim turned and unceremoniously hurled the bloke standing opposite him to the ground. And so I went for the forward nearest to me. A newspaper report the next day said, 'Blakeway and Jarrett should never play first-class rugby again.' Quite a start to my Gloucester career!

I shall always retain happy memories of the Kingsholm crowd, so critical at times and yet always capable of lifting morale when the occasion demanded. One of the great games of recent years featured the touring Taranaki provincial side from New Zealand, which included All Blacks skipper Graham Mourie and the match-winning international scrum-half, Dave Loveridge.

The supporters were an inspiration that night. I had just returned after yet another spell of injury and played out of my skin for the club. So did the other Gloucester

122

forwards and eventually a visiting side which has often given the British Lions a run for its money in New Zealand was well beaten.

Even Dickie Trimble, a real Kingsholm character, would have had a job to make himself heard during the Taranaki match. As a young Gloucester player, I soon became accustomed to the occasional sound of a trumpet from somewhere in among the crowd on the old changing-room side of the pitch. If we were performing badly and the spectators fell quiet, the strains of the Last Post would suddenly drift across Kingsholm. It caused much amusement in that part of the ground, although it wasn't always the sort of encouragement needed by the players. I remember one night when Bristol, including John Pullin and that aggressive loose-head prop Mike 'The Greek' Fry, took our long-standing ground record in a typically close and hard-fought derby match. Inevitably, Dickie performed the Last Post just before the end.

Afterwards, you could have cut the atmosphere in our dressing room with a knife. 'If I find that bloke with the trumpet, I'll stick it down his bloody throat,' I muttered. It was a long time before I discovered Dickie's identity and realized he had no trumpet – somehow, he was able to produce the sound of the instrument by blowing through his hands.

Bristol matches invariably bring the best out of Gloucester as well. I shall never forget an occasion in April 1977 when we spoiled the farewell Memorial Ground appearances for Bristol of that outstanding old England forward David Rollitt and another fine stalwart, David Tyler. Between them, Rollitt and Tyler had played more than 800 games for the club and, understandably, Bristol were keen to make the most of the occasion.

But it was a match when everything went right for Gloucester. We won 34–9 – the biggest victory margin in the long history of fixtures between the sides – and even Fidler picked up the ball on one occasion and charged almost the length of the field.

One of Gloucester's great characters is John Fidler, the Great White Shark as I used to called him. He has become the Great White Whale since retirement. I actually knew Fidler when he was thin! That was back in 1966 when we played together for Cheltenham colts – and I've a picture that proves it.

More seriously, 'Fids' has done a sterling job since taking charge of physical fitness at Gloucester. But he is a ruthless taskmaster. Trouble is that he learned all the dodges when he was a player – and knows what hurts. 'For a bloke who was never fit in his life, you're a swine,' I told him during a real slogging session one night. He was totally unmoved and flogged us even more. With men like Fidler around, Gloucester's future is secure.

Gloucester, as I have said, rely very much on a thriving local rugby set-up to supply their players.

My last game in a Gloucester shirt was an exhilarating John Player Cup semi-final against Bath at Kingsholm. We lost 12–11 and a fascinating statistic was that our prop Richard Pascall and lock Dick Burn were the only players who were not products of the Combination system. Skipper John Orwin, another import, was required for duty with the RAF team at Twickenham on the same afternoon.

That match, incidentally, provided a demonstration of all that is best in English club rugby. Both sides were wholly committed to winning and, with a huge crowd filling the ground, the tension was considerable. Yet, from start to finish, there wasn't a single penalty for foul play.

The game also underlined the transformation which Kingsholm rugby has undergone since the dreadful 1982 season. Contrary to all tradition, Gloucester was now adopting a fifteen-man style – and doing it successfully as well. Even though I pleaded with our scrum-half Marcus Hannaford to put a couple in the air against Bath, he still kept running. In the end it was ironical that Bath, renowned for their open approach to the game, should beat us by playing the old Gloucester-style ten-man rugby. Although we lost, I told the lads in the dressing room, 'Gentlemen, it's been a pleasure to be involved in such a fine game.' Not a bad way to bid farewell, I suppose.

Many great players graced the Gloucester side during my years at Kingsholm. But no man was bigger than the club. You might be an England player and go on a British Lions tour. But woe betide anyone who thought he was any more important than the average bloke in the United.

The Gloucester lads always found a way of cutting you down to size. In my last season, someone took to placing a baby's dummy on my peg in the dressing room. 'Come on, Dad,' they used to say. Steve Boyle, who moved on from Gloucester to Moseley in the 1984–85 season, suffered unmerciful stick after touring with the Lions. Henceforth, he was known as 'Lenny' after the television ventriloquist's dummy.

At Gloucester, therefore, you were only as good as your last game. At one time, I had quite a long stint in the United team with three more internationals, Gordon Sargent, John Fidler and scrum-half Peter Kingston.

Men like the talkative Mickey Booth, the philosophical Terry Hopson and bustling John Bayliss sum up Gloucester rugby for me. Bayliss was a real thrust and bang merchant in the centre who put the fear of God into any opposition. Like me, he broke his neck playing at Kingsholm – in a fairly innocuous tackle with Neil Bennett, the England fly-half who was then with Loughborough Colleges. Gloucester has a reputation for a fairly rough-and-ready approach to rugby, but the casualty record book of club doctor Tom Durkin shows that, over the years, there have been far more serious injuries to home players than visiting teams.

Of the lesser-known players, Mike Potter is typical of the dedicated Kingsholm man. The Yellow Hammer of Coney Hill, they called him. Big and broad-shouldered, he was unmistakable with his bald head. He was enormously strong and the type of selfless grafter which every good team needs. If an opponent moved, he hammered him.

The Kingsholm faithful still rhapsodize about that John Player Cup semi-final victory over London Welsh in 1972 and the part played by Potter. He might have been overawed at the prospect of standing opposite Lions' star

Mervyn Davies in the line-out. But Yellow Hammer wasn't interested in reputations. He had a fabulous game at no. 8.

Potter had his own, highly effective way of tackling. Somehow, he was able to wrap his huge arms around an opponent, fling him over and dump him on the turf on your side. The rest of the forwards would then surge over the top and the ball popped up as sweetly as you could wish. It happened hundreds of times.

I learned to appreciate Potter during a pre-season club trial. There was no doubt in my mind that I had firm control of the ball and could set up a smooth ruck. Suddenly I was in Potter's iron grip, launched into orbit and then aware of what seemed like a thousand feet marching over me.

Potter still turns up regularly at Kingsholm, although sadly his career was cut short by a dodgy knee. He's a super chap – scratch him and you would find gold. I had good reason to be grateful to him one night when I received a bang on the head and sought the refuge of a distant corner in the Kingsholm clubhouse.

It was bitterly cold outside and like a hothouse indoors, with beer swilling all over the floor, a blanket of smoke and people packed shoulder to shoulder throughout – a typical clubhouse scene. Ros was due to pick me up and understandably looked anxious when she arrived at the door. Potter didn't know her but realized something was wrong and made a point of sorting out the problem, steering her safely through the room to where I sat feeling distinctly groggy. A small gesture perhaps, which he probably won't even remember – but the sort of thing which makes you appreciate Gloucester Rugby Club and its people.

12

Room for Improvement

One of my fruit-grower friends always stresses that, to obtain a good crop of apples, an ailing tree needs drastic pruning – a bit of straightforward logic which applies to English rugby. The Grand Slam side of 1980, England's first since 1957, came together more by chance than anything else. And unless the Rugby Union brush off the cobwebs and engineer a complete overhaul of the structure of the game in this country, it will be another twenty-three years – and, more likely, a lot more – before we pop the champagne corks once again.

The Scots have introduced leagues and, while their international record was poor in 1985, they will flourish again as a result. In Ireland, the provincial and schools' set-up produced class threequarters and a wonderful back row from nowhere in recent times; and the Welsh are happy to pluck the best talent from the most powerful club network in the world.

So where do we stand in England? The Mallaby Report suggested wholesale change some years ago – and was ignored. More recently, John Burgess also turned his considerable business talents to the possibility of establishing a new, workable structure. His findings, too, continue to gather ·dust at RFU headquarters, Twickenham.

Everything about English rugby is wrong. Win a place in the national side and you have a permanent feeling that there are certain things you must be seen to be doing on the field. Every team needs organization – but there are times when you yearn just to go out and play and let instinct do the rest.

I am convinced we must establish a system which allows a man like Wade Dooley to find his way more easily to the top. Dooley wore the England shirt in 1985 simply because national coach Dick Greenwood happened to be from his club, Preston Grasshoppers, and believed the player had the physical capabilities to cope with international rugby.

In reality, Dooley achieved the equivalent of going straight from a point-to-point meeting to winning the Derby. But his route up would have been far less dramatic if there had been a sensible league structure throughout the country which encouraged both club and individual player to progress.

The problem is that everyone in England is too busy protecting his own self-interest. The north and the west fight in the main to perpetuate the County Championship; the Midlands by and large don't want to know county rugby and favour divisional competition; the south seems to be split in all directions.

Divisional rugby is certainly acceptable when major tour sides are in this country. But, as a recently retired senior player, I am sure that a strong system of leagues, giving the small clubs a chance to escape the shackles of traditional fixture lists, is an absolute essential.

The John Player Cup has proved the value of club competition. Had anyone outside the north of England heard of Gosforth, Morley and Orrell before knock-out rugby was introduced?

My argument would, of course, mean the end of the County Championship as a major event in the English rugby calendar. And that suggestion might seem surprising from someone brought up in a hotbed of the county game.

Certainly I was proud to help Gloucestershire beat Somerset in front of a large and enthusiastic crowd at Twickenham in 1984. In all honesty, however, it only boiled down to a meeting between a team drawn from Bristol and Gloucester and another exclusively from Bath.

Nottingham provided the entire Notts, Lincs and Derby team in the final a year later.

England selectors will learn as much as they need to know from watching top-class club competition. From that, they can stage a realistic international trial. I mean no disrespect to clubs in my area such as Lydney and Stroud. The truth is, however, that they do not provide players who are likely to walk straight into the national side. Anyone with the talent to reach this level can only hope to do so via Gloucester or Bristol.

At Gloucester, it infuriated us a while back that Leicester, whose players ignore the County Championship, was being described as England's top club. Our overall results certainly looked inferior. But the fact of the matter was that Gloucester had not put out a full side for weeks because of county, divisional and other representative calls. For once, our best term faced the Tigers – and mauled them by more than 30 points.

English rugby would benefit enormously if much of the sponsorship cash pumped into the county game could be directed to the clubs instead. This would upgrade grounds, install more efficient training areas and perhaps give players a better insight into how their own individual training methods can be improved.

It should be possible to find enough financial backing for a club league to ensure that Gloucester, for instance, played Gosforth home and away every season. The trips would include an overnight stay in each case, introducing another small way of preparing players for the final leap into international rugby.

The argument that the geography of England makes league competition difficult to establish is really a red herring. The majority of clubs would still be involved on a regional basis at lower levels. And travel has never been that much of a barrier to the top player – Maurice Colclough, when he was in London, used to delight in pointing out that he was still closer to Paris than if he had been back home in his French base of Angoulême.

At the moment, we are hopelessly shackled by tradition.

129

What we require is firm direction from Twickenham and insistence from the clubs as to what course shall be taken.

When he was president of the RFU, Dickie Jeeps set something of a precedent by coming more into the public eye and pushing his own views. Since then, others have followed suit. The problem is that something which may have been a sensible idea one year is knocked down the next. This really is no way to run affairs. ICI or British Leyland have a managing director who dictates how his company will operate perhaps years ahead. We need full-time officers at Twickenham with the same sort of muscle – not dozens of people all demanding their own little slice of the cake. The old school-tie argument that what was good for rugby in the past should still apply is outdated. But this sort of thinking lives on.

Nothing more accurately illustrates the farcical structure of the English game than the method of qualifying for the John Player Cup in the South-West. Instead of simply stating that Bath, Bristol and Gloucester deserve automatic entry into the third round of the competition, they are required each year to run the gauntlet of a regional merit table which is absolutely loaded in favour of the sides in Cornwall and Devon.

While Plymouth and Camborne prospered in my final year through home-and-away fixtures against struggling Exeter and Redruth, Gloucester was judged on its record in five games – two each against Bath and Bristol, which were all lost, and one at Exeter, where victory on the last day of the season earned the consolation of a place in next year's first round with the best junior clubs.

But for that Exeter win, there would have been no cup rugby in 1985–86 for Gloucester – and we were beaten by a single point in the semi-final of 1984–85 to the eventual champion Bath. How ludicrous. In previous seasons, Gloucester, Bath and Bristol have all fallen foul of the South-West Merit Table and failed to qualify in one season. Surely, someone at Twickenham must realize it's a nonsense.

Let's establish a proper league system throughout the country and stop tinkering with the idea of competitive rugby by establishing merit tables based on long-standing fixture lists.

One job in rugby I could never begin to attempt is that of the referee. The poor bloke is a loser from the start because he has little chance of satisfying every one of thirty players whose individual ambition at the start of each game is to make him look a bit of a Charlie!

The ability of this one man will determine whether your game is going to be enjoyable sport or a disorganized fight. The sooner the authorities make his role marginally easier by giving touch judges the power of intervention in club games, the better.

Clive Norling has the perfect refereeing credentials – he is a strong character and has a refreshing sense of humour as well. He has a feel for the game too – an absolute essential – and so players always respect his decisions.

When the front rows are battling for supremacy early in a game, Norling invariably blows his whistle and delivers a brief lecture in his booming Welsh voice 'If you drop it, we re-scrum. If it goes down again, I penalize. It's up to you.'

Gary Pearce and I were having a real go one day when we met in the traditional East Midlands-Barbarians match at Northampton. 'Gentlemen, I am telling you now, sort it out yourselves and keep the scrum up or I will deal with it. And this goes for next week as well.' (Reference to another game we were due to play.)

Fair enough, I decided, you're the guv'nor. And the game progressed smoothly after that. Norling is something of a showman – and there's always room for such characters. But I do feel there is a danger of overstepping the mark.

It happened when England was playing Rumania at Twickenham for the first time. Another Welshman, Derek Bevan, did a fair job with the whistle that day. But Norling, acting as touch judge, still stamped his personality on the game – and infuriated the England players.

We had started the match well and built a good lead. But in the second half the Rumanians were kicking their

131

penalties and edging back into contention. And every time the ball soared between our posts, a voice echoed across the ground: 'It's o . . . ver.' I thought at first it was someone in the crowd. But then I realized it was Norling. As the pressure on us was mounting considerably at that stage, I could cheerfully have walked o . . . ver and punched him on the nose! All he had to do was raise his flag in the normal manner. Play the part of a showman on occasions by all means – but this was hardly the time and place.

One of the best decisions in recent years has been to appoint neutral referees for Test matches. Frenchman Francis Palmade proved the value of this when he came out to South Africa during England's 1984 tour and did an excellent job.

Sadly, Norman Sanson, another fine referee, was shamefully treated in 1977. He was nominated for the France-Ireland game, which was to bring the home side the Grand Slam. But the French feared Sanson's reputation as a disciplinarian because they had several rough-necks in their pack. They refused to accept the Scotsman – and the International Board, to their eternal discredit, bowed to pressure. Refereeing was set back years, especially when the disillusioned Sanson retired shortly afterwards.

I confess here and now that I have played a full part in conning referees. At a line-out, for instance, there are a dozen or more possible offences. The hard-pressed ref checks that spacing between players is right, that no one is closing the gap and there is no lifting . . . but does he look at what's happening on the ground?

One of my favourite tricks, usually to thwart a successful line-out jumper, was simply to tread on his foot just at the moment the ball left the thrower's hands. It's perfect because the referee can't see, the rival forward can't jump – and your victim is usually so mad that he reacts and concedes a vital penalty. Game, set and match to Blakeway.

I recall procuring a vital penalty for England in Stellenbosch, South Africa. The home side had a fairly stroppy

132

winger and so I deliberately ran into him in open play and roughed him up a bit. Naturally, he reacted – and we collected three points which clinched victory.

Of course, it's easy to get caught out yourself. The sparks used to fly when Gloucester played Leicester and I came up against my old Kingsholm comrade-in-arms Robin Cowling. During the first of these games, Leicester forced a scrum early on inside our 22 and, contrary to all logic, Cowling deliberately collapsed it with a real thud. The referee pointed at me and awarded a penalty to Leicester and Peter Wheeler, who was doing the goal-kicking for the Tigers in those days, gratefully notched three points. Cowling ran away laughing.

The same thing happened to Austin Sheppard almost as soon as he came on to replace injured Fran Cotton against Wales at Cardiff in 1981. There was a scrum near our posts with a Welsh put-in and down to the ground we went. It was not Sheppard's fault. Ian Stephens had done the dirty on us that time. Incidentally, it cost England three points – the difference between glory and disaster in a match we lost 21–19.

Players have to suffer video films on training nights which make it glaringly obvious where things went wrong on the previous Saturday. It wouldn't be a bad idea for referees' societies to use the same system much more. Referees can't be expected to see everything but at least there would be an opportunity to sit down and discuss possible ways of improving performance.

We must have more consistency. Everyone agreed that the sending-off by Welsh referee Winston Jones of hookers Peter Wheeler and Mark McBain in the 1984 game between the Midlands and Australia was a travesty. They were involved in nothing more than a minor skirmish. A few days later, however, the same referee merely issued a warning in a BBC Rugby Special game when Welsh international forward Richard Moriarty, of Swansea, laid out rival second-row Barry Clegg with a swinging punch. A crazy case of double standards.

One of my rules was not to allow a referee to rush things if I wasn't ready. In pressure situations, the object was never to go down early in the scrum unless there was a chance of a quick feed from your own scrum-half and a rapid clearance. This offered valuable time to catch your breath. Conversely, on the opposition line, the idea was to catch them while they were suffering in defence and form the scrum as rapidly as possible.

Seemingly small matters like this can ultimately mean the difference between winning and losing a game. Similarly, it's wise to hold things up a bit if one of your side is trying to shrug off a knock. Wade Dooley was crocked against Rumania in his international debut but bravely continued to hobble to the next set-piece. 'Go down son, and take your water,' I advised. 'Don't be a hero.'

Coaches vary enormously in their approach and attitude to the game. And one of the best I encountered was Mike Davis who was in charge of England's 1980 Grand Slam side.

Admittedly, Davis had the good fortune to have an exceptional squad of players. But he still needed to get the best out of his troops and this was achieved by recognizing that highly experienced characters like Fran Cotton, Tony Neary, Steve Smith, Peter Wheeler, Mike Slemen and Dusty Hare could offer expert knowledge and advice in very specialist areas of the game.

Davis had coached the England schools' side and the under-23s, where in each case it was necessary to dictate a playing policy. At the very senior level, however, he was astute enough to be a listener and yet, at the same time, still have the final say – and this was a significant factor in the team's success.

Dick Greenwood's philosophy was entirely different. He came in bursting with enthusiasm and new ideas, which included the monitoring of fitness through a series of tests on the athletics track. But the South African tour was something of a shambles and, by the end of the 1985 season, I felt he had become rather disillusioned.

I have never understood why the Rugby Union consistently ignore coaches with proven records of success at club level. Chalkie White had a wonderful run at Leicester and is held in the highest regard by men like Peter

Wheeler – but he did not stand any messing about from authority and clearly this radical stance was too much for the RFU.

Des Seabrook, outstandingly successful with the north, Lancashire and Sale, Dave Robinson, also of the north, and Bath's Jack Rowell were all overlooked when it came to finding a substitute for Greenwood in New Zealand. Rugby could learn from soccer in this instance – you won't find Manchester United going to the nearest public school to find a new manager. United decide who is the best for the job, irrespective of background, and go out and get him.

13

Agony and Ecstasy

Mike Burton and Fran Cotton were Lions in every sense of the word. Indomitable characters with hearts of oak. I witnessed high points in the careers of both; and yet I was also present at very private moments when it seemed the whole world had caved in around them.

Burton's life hit rock bottom when he contemplated the humiliation of his dismissal in the Battle of Brisbane. He has been a comedian all his life. But there were no wise-cracks during that crisis and I watched him suffer.

Perhaps more than anyone else on the Australian tour, I knew the serious side of a prop forward who put in so many hours of sweat and toil over the hills of Church-down, Gloucester. He was never that fast and couldn't do a press-up if you paid him. But he was exceptionally strong and, as I have already indicated, possibly without parallel in my experience as a front-row technician.

If Cotton had not resisted a move to loose head during the early part of his career, 'Burto' would undoubtedly have won more than seventeen caps. His disciplinary record didn't help. And he was drawn to controversy like a magnet. But the England or British Lions shirt was always worn with pride.

The same is certainly true of Fran, the player they called 'Jaws' on account of his massive bulk and protuberant chin.

His nadir was the Lions' tour of South Africa in 1980, a matter of weeks after we had shared in the exultation of England's Grand Slam success. As the broken rib curtailed my active service as a Lion to just seventy-four minutes, I was to spend a great deal of time with Fran before and after his heart-attack scare in Stellenbosch.

After taking part in the victory over Natal in Durban – the third match of the tour – he suffered terribly in the heat as did all the players. He was a replacement for the fourth game against a South African XV at Potchefstroom but his legs had been swelling and causing considerable discomfort (major surgery was necessary later that year to sort out a varicose vein problem) and so Fran went straight back to the hotel after the match. Fran knew, however, that time was running out fast and that if he didn't play in the sixth tour match against a South African Rugby Federation XV at the Danie Craven Stadium, Stellenbosch, Welshman Clive Williams would claim the loose-head spot in the first Test four days later.

I guessed he wasn't really fit to play. And this was confirmed subsequently by lock Allan Martin, who described how the England forward was literally pushing the swelling up his legs in order to get his boots on. This shows the extent of an ambition to add to the Lions' honours he won in South Africa six years earlier and again in New Zealand in 1977.

When eventually Fran walked off after half an hour, I thought he had broken a rib. But he was rushed to the local hospital with an oxygen mask held over his face and later Noel Murphy brought the news that it was suspected Fran had suffered a heart attack. None of us was able to comprehend that this disaster could strike such a strong and fit individual.

As I was off tour, the management detailed me to go to the hospital that evening and stay with Fran while everyone else went to the match dinner. When I entered the ward, I saw this huge figure lying motionless – and he was extremely upset.

It transpired that the hospital authorities had stupidly told Fran that he had suffered a heart attack. So here was a man stranded thousands of miles from home fearing he might never see his wife Pat and fourteen-week-old daughter Rachael again. I could understand his feelings

137

– my own son back home in Gloucestershire was only six weeks old at the time.

Not long after, I hit the roof when I went to sit with Fran for a second time and discovered a whole posse of pressmen crowding around the bed and attempting to fire questions. Although no one back at the ground let on where Fran had been taken, certain Fleet Street journalists took it upon themselves to seek him out and – even though the poor guy was still having his heartbeat monitored on a machine – infiltrate the ward. I ejected the lot of them in double-quick time.

This was by no means the end of the drama. There was now the very real possibility that Pat Cotton would listen to the news at home and hear that Fran had suffered a heart attack. Desperate telephone calls took place and fortunately this was avoided.

The next day I accompanied Fran some forty miles to Groote Schuur Hospital, Cape Town, the world-famous establishment where Dr Christian Barnard had performed his first heart transplant. Fran tells the lovely story of how he was being whisked from test to test and passed the great man in the corridor. On seeing the British Lions' tracksuit, Barnard stopped and asked what was wrong.

'I've no idea,' said Cotton. 'Don't worry,' came the reply. 'If you need a new one then I'm sure we can arrange it for you upstairs.' I told Fran myself, 'They would never find one big enough to go in there anyway.' By that stage, thank goodness, he was able to offer a wry smile. The doctors were beginning to realize that it had all been a very unpleasant false alarm.

Syd Millar called a press conference and really laid into those present for what had happened in the hospital ward. I admired John Mason, of the *Daily Telegraph*, for the stand which he took at this juncture. 'Some of us have more respect for the dignity of man,' he said. 'We are here to report the rugby and nothing else.'

Happily, Fran made a full recovery. This man-mountain achieved so much in his career – playing for both England and the Lions as a tight head and loose head and captaining his country as well. He would jut out a

138

huge chin and fend off anything that could be hurled in his direction.

The 1980 Lions had the capability to win the series – I am sure of that. But injuries and non-availabilities were absolutely crucial. Neither Tony Neary nor Fergus Slattery was able to travel and Paul Ringer, who would have revelled on the hard grounds, had blotted his copybook at Twickenham. So when Stuart Lane was invalided out of the trip in the very first minute, we were left without a 'flier' – and the problems grew from there.

South Africa was also so well prepared. They had waited six years to avenge a 3–1 drubbing by Willie-John McBride's splendid side and built methodically towards the Tests with matches against the Jaguars (virtually the Argentinian side) as well as trying various combinations against the Lions.

Were the Lions wrong to select only eight members of England's Grand Slam side? Probably so. I can't help wondering how many Welshmen would have travelled if their side had swept all before them in the International Championship.

Paul Dodge proved the point when he went out as replacement and ended up playing a leading role in the solitary Test victory in Pretoria. I also felt John Scott was particularly unfortunate not to be chosen – although it was almost inevitable that politics would be an influence and cost somebody a place.

The Lions undoubtedly paid for not learning the lessons of the 1977 tour of New Zealand, when coach John Dawes was criticized for making too many demands on his players in training. From our experiences at Vanderbijlpark, I can vouch for the fact that Noel Murphy compounded the error in 1980.

Even though my tour was so abbreviated, however, I would not have missed the experience for anything. To have the dream of playing in a Test destroyed so abruptly was a bitter blow. But I can say I was a Lion.

When I look back on my career, I can't help but feel how amazingly lucky I have been. Playing for a premier club like Gloucester, for instance, opened the door for England under-23 and Australian tour opportunities early on. My neck was broken – but not badly enough to lead to disaster. And above all I was so fortunate to have been introduced to senior international rugby just at the birth of one of the truly great eras of the game in this country.

Although I didn't fully appreciate it at the time, I was the addition to a group of seven world-class forwards. My feet may have been up around Gordon Sargent's chest when we practised scrummaging for the very first time at Bisham Abbey, but after that it was easy.

All coach Mike Davis wanted me to do was tie things down and let the others operate. The players didn't demand anything fancy from me. 'Stand in scrum, stand in line-out' was Fran's dictum. And for much of the time that's exactly what I did.

It was just like joining a well-established club. England had abandoned the hit-and-miss selection policy of the 1970s, although it's interesting to reflect that they didn't get it quite right against the All Blacks in the November of the 1979–80 season.

The North, it will be recalled, had hammered the New Zealanders at Otley on the Saturday before the Twickenham international. There were rumours that the national XV had been picked beforehand – and certainly the exclusion of Roger Uttley, who had done so much to nullify the line-out threat of Andy Haden, supported that view.

In the end, England's 10–9 defeat by the tourists restored Uttley to England's blind-side flank and brought another Lancashire lad, fly-half John Horton, into the fray. In all, there were nine Lancashire representatives. No wonder I was viewed as the 'country bumpkin from "Glawster".'

It was an enormous advantage, of course, that the majority of the team had played so much together – and known success virtually all the way. All I did was tag along. Often, this was literally what happened because, although I tried hard enough to get involved as much as possible, there were occasions when I was charging .

140

upfield and doing little more than watch these guys play their own game.

Bill Beaumont, as I have said, was the driving force who put my international career on a firm footing. He gave 100 per cent at every scrum – and 110 per cent if there was any semblance of pressure from the opposition.

Since 1980, there have been critics who said he failed to change tactics quickly enough to meet a particular situation. But I would never fault him on that score. A skipper can only do so much – in the end, it's up to the individuals around him to take crucial decisions.

Another great strength in the Grand Slam side lay in our confidence in each other's ability. Bill established a level of communication between players, coach and selectors which had not been achieved before – or since. The 24–9 win over Ireland was a marvellous start – but it merely had the effect of making us redouble our efforts and improve before the tougher games against France and Wales.

Each individual was a competitor. Fran Cotton would have hated to lose to anyone at tiddlywinks and Peter Wheeler, the other member of the front-row union, had the same attitude. Uttley and Neary had a phenomenal season, complementing one another perfectly, and our backs were even more effective once the combination of Clive Woodward and Paul Dodge – again a partnership of vividly contrasting talents – was established.

I might so easily have been one of England's countless 'here today, gone tomorrow' players. But in the elite company of the 1980 side, I could hardly avoid playing well.

It saddens me that England has not followed up 1980 with further success. There is no shortage of manpower in this country. But our structure of competition does not achieve enough in bringing through players of top calibre.

The argument is put forward that modern youngsters have a far greater range of activities to choose from and, of course, this is true. But New Zealand has consistently managed to stay at the very top as a rugby nation and still unearth star performers in cricket, athletics, tennis and other sports.

We must have a system which somehow links the players from Penzance and Newlyn with those at West Hartlepool and ensures the best talent finds a way through.

England must also shrug off once again the rigid type of coaching which led to a South-West XV playing the All Blacks at Bristol in a style totally in conflict with the skills of the selected side. There have been numerous occasions when I felt an England team had talent – but the players were not allowed to play. Often, you were too concerned about being seen to do the right things rather than acting with imagination and risking the odd mistake.

England's lack of imagination was apparent in a disappointing 1984 season when the Scots' approach was far more fluid and reaped a rich reward as a result. Sometimes, too much emphasis is placed on the set-piece. But the scrum is not a game within a game. The aim is to win the ball and let others take over.

The Australians certainly underlined our shortcomings later in 1984 with a refreshing brand of attacking rugby which earned a clean sweep against the four home countries. The New Zealanders play with that extra element of freedom and imagination as well.

We might compete on level terms with them in the tight. But the All Blacks have five front forwards who can act as auxiliary back-row men when necessary and a marauding back row who are also wonderfully mobile and creative. Second-row Gary Whetton, for instance, is a tremendous athlete. When he played for the Welsh Rugby Union President's XV against Wales at Cardiff in 1984, he made one break in which he accelerated away from fly-half Malcolm Dacey.

Let's hope that in future seasons England adopts a slightly less regimented approach to rugby. I quite agree with John Carleton's observation that performances in South Africa in 1984 were an embarrassment and that something radical has to be done.

To an extent, therefore, I can accept coach Dick Greenwood's philosophy that monitoring our performance levels over various runs and exercises before the 1985 internationals would benefit the side. A fitter rugby player is likely to operate faster and more competitively over a longer period.

But a man who is super-fit and quick over 400 metres isn't necessarily the best player for a particular position. Only the expert analytical mind of a coach can decide that. Peronally, I found that slipping straight into a few hundred press-ups did not help an awful lot when it came to playing for England. The whole training programme was based too much on a fitness slog and, slowly but surely, that vital element of flair and initiative was being squeezed out.

They tell me that French prop Jean-Pierre Garuet – sent off for gouging by Clive Norling against Ireland in 1984 – was quite outstanding in New Zealand. Yet he's a real roly-poly figure – and I guarantee he could not have run 100 metres in eleven seconds for Dick Greenwood.

New Zealand skipper Graham Mourie said that no British international selectors would have picked the All Blacks prop Rod Spiers because he wasn't fast enough around the field. But he suited Mourie's requirements. And no greater accolade is required.

Let's take a leaf out of the Irish book and put a little more adventure back into our game. The players there so obviously enjoy their rugby and the Irish nation as a whole are so committed that even the ball boys and the match doctor seem to be competitive at Lansdowne Road.

Rugby is changing – and so are the laws. My retirement could well have come at just the right time in some respects because there is no doubt the destructive, scrum-maging specialist may be redundant in no time at all.

I am the first to recognize that something has to be done to reduce the frequency of collapsed scrums. Not many players are hurt in this way in first-class club rugby or internationals. Forwards have the strength and experience to cope.

But that isn't the point. At lower levels, it is a danger. Far too many youngsters have suffered critical injuries in the last few years and the game must alter to reduce these incidences to a minimum.

One solution put forward quite seriously was that props should not go lower than the referee's hips. But how tall is the referee? Give me a titch like Laurie Prideaux any time!

The compromise is that shoulders must not go beneath waist height – and that's worth a try. This has tended to happen in France already where the idea seems to be that, as long as the ball goes in and gets away, that's good enough. There are not many instances of strikes against the head in French rugby. But that element of competition has to a great extent disappeared from rugby already. How often does BBC commentator Bill McLaren rhapsodize about a hooker stealing the ball in an international scrum? Not very frequently. If it does happen, it invariably takes the successful team so much by surprise that no advantage accrues.

Injuries, of course, have taken a sizeable chunk out of my career. And it is comforting to know that the sport has been adopting a far more responsible attitude in this respect in recent years.

International Board regulations now bar a player who suffers concussion from returning to the game too soon. That didn't apply in Bill Beaumont's day and there seems little doubt that his retirement in 1982 was accelerated by returning too soon after being kicked on the head during a trip to France with Lancashire. He was booted again in his final international against Scotland before trudging off for the last time in a County Championship final.

I wonder if my broken neck might have been detected a little quicker these days, although admittedly I did my best to conceal the injury when it happened. At least Bill and I are still around to enjoy a few years as grandstand critics.

Rugby has given me so much. Although I left school without a qualification to my name, I have received a privileged education since then touring all over the world and simply observing. Nowadays I pass on the sage advice offered to me in my early days as a bit of a rugby tearaway. 'Say nowt, do nowt and you can't go far wrong!'

There have been so many extraordinary characters. I can see the face of giant Scottish lock Alan Tomes when we were all weighed at the start of the Lions' tour in 1980 and he was promptly put on a diet!

I think of Ray Gravell, who risked life and limb a thousand times on behalf of Wales but wouldn't sit out in the South African sun because he feared it was bad for him; and Irish full-back Rodney O'Donnell, another neck-injury victim, who smoked the foulest cigarettes which have ever been manufactured.

The Grand Slam side were all a great bunch. And there were unforgettable personalities in England's tour side to South Africa in 1984. One of the quiet men of the trip was scrum-half Richard Hill – or Duracell, as we called him. The lad had copper-coloured hair, black shorts and the ability to go on and on for ever!

The noisiest player I ever met was also on that trip – winger David Trick. As a snorer, Fran Cotton was loud and merited his nickname King Kip. But Trick should be reported to the noise-abatement people.

I had heard rumours about his remarkable snoring but didn't worry about it too much when we roomed together before the second international in Johannesburg. Trick, to be fair, advised me to get to sleep first – but I couldn't. Suddenly, this awful din started up and I was convinced he was having me on. But he wasn't. It continued like a giant chain-saw all night.

There is no doubt that 1980 was my year. One minute I was training with Gloucester hardly daring to think I might play rugby again after breaking my neck. The next I was wearing the white shirt of England in one of the finest sides the country has ever produced. But for Fran's insistence – 'You don't leave this field when we are ten minutes from history' – I would have missed that final ecstatic moment when we clinched the Grand Slam.

'You'll have to wait for me to catch you up at the scrums,' I gasped. 'We will,' came the reply.

Rugby Career: Dates

Year	Event	Venue	Result	Score
1950	Philip John Blakeway born at Cheltenham on 31 December			
1968	Joined Cheltenham Rugby Club			
1971	Moved to Gloucester RFC			
1973	England under-23s v. Japan	Twickenham	Won	19–10
1975	England tour of Australia			
1977	Broke neck playing for Gloucester			
1980	England debut v. Ireland	Twickenham	Won	24–9
	France v. England	Paris	Won	17–13
	England v. Wales	Twickenham	Won	9–8
	Scotland v. England	Murrayfield	Won	30–18
	British Lions tour, South Africa, cut short by broken rib			
1981	Wales v. England	Cardiff	Lost	19–21
	England v. Scotland	Twickenham	Won	23–17
	Ireland v. England	Dublin	Won	10–6
	England v. France	Twickenham	Lost	12–16
	Captain, South and South-West Counties v. Australia	Gloucester		
1982	England v. Ireland	Twickenham	Lost	15–16
	France v. England	Paris	Won	27–15
	England v. Wales	Twickenham	Won	17–7
	England tour of Canada and United States			
	Captain, South and South-West Counties v. Fiji	Camborne		
1983	Captain, South and South-West Counties v. All Blacks	Bristol		
1984	England v. Ireland	Twickenham	Won	12–9
	France v. England	Paris	Lost	18–32
	England v. Wales	Twickenham	Lost	15–24
	England tour, South Africa			
	South Africa v. England	Port Elizabeth	Lost	15–33

1985	England *v*. Rumania	Twickenham	Won	22–15
	England *v*. France	Twickenham	Drawn	9–9
	England *v*. Scotland	Twickenham	Won	10–7
	Ireland *v*. England	Dublin	Lost	10–13